LEGACY PLAYBOOK

Unearthing eternal echoes and unveiling the tapestry of legacy

KELLY MARKEY

First published by Markey Writing Academy 2023

Find us on Facebook @KellyMarkeyAuthor and Instagram @Author_Kelly_Markey

AUTHOR.KELLY.MARKEY.

Hardcover ISBN: 978-0-6451968-3-2

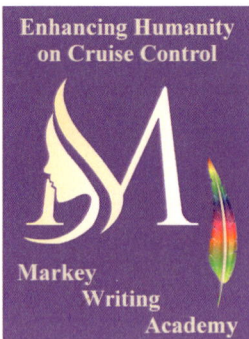

Enhancing Humanity on Cruise Control

Markey Writing Academy

Cover Design: Markey Writing Academy

Layout: Markey Writing Academy

Typesetting: Markey Writing Academy

Markey Writing Academy
Central Coast, New South Wales Australia, 2250
www.kellymarkey.com

This playbook is dedicated to all the history makers and legacy builders. You are crafting a world on purpose... the future generation salutes you!

Table of Contents

Kudos for Legacy Playbook

If you've ever found yourself in the state of contemplation and asking the questions "What will people remember about me when I die?" Or better yet "Will people even remember me after I leave the planet?" then this book by the Amazing Kelly Markey is a must read. Not because it answers the questions you're asking; but rather because it puts the power in your hands to ensure that your life will be recalled with fondness and potentially used as a compass for those who will step in the footprints you have left behind. This life guiding book further enables you to curate exactly what people will always recall about your journey on this earth.

I advise you, the reader to embark on this life enhancing read with and open mind, embrace this book as a tool, undertake each activity with honesty and transparency by taking your lead from the author who becomes vulnerable through her writing. As you turn the pages of Legacy Playbook, may it turn the pages of your life into stories that will live long after you have drawn your last breath.

Rachel Biggar: Radio & Television Broadcaster, Johannesburg, South Africa

This book is highly recommended for anyone who wants to build a strong legacy. There are powerful tips which show that creating a conducive environment is very important to be successful in this endeavour. A summary of the content in this book is that all success lies largely with the individual as Kelly makes it clear that setting personal goals, self-introspection, positive attitude and character building are the secrets to success in legacy building.

Jennifer Ndlovu: Woman in Technology, Implementation Consultation, Agilyx Group, Bulawayo, Zimbabwe.

Kelly has produced a book that will help many dig deep and challenge their perspective of who they are, open ways to develop as a person and encourage the pursuit of self-development and growth. Each reader will find life changing words that cut away the old thinking and open them up to new ways of thinking and acting! This book is encouraging and challenging, pearls of wisdom throughout the pages.

Gai Carman, Wife, Mother, Grandmother, Financial Counsellor and Community Services Manager, Dubbo, Australia

I highly recommend this book for those seeking to enlighten themselves about authentically enhancing their character and defining a legacy. Kelly Markey will validate the expression of life as you work through these pages.

Radio Station, Washington DC, USA.

Foreword

Kelly Markey. Profound change. The award-winning author, I believe, created just that with her writing for the Legacy Playbook. Profound change in one's self. From the Preface, my attention was captured in a snare of interest. From artful connotations to emotionally evoking personal experiences, life-altering scenarios and spiritually moving quotes.

There is no way that I can conclude that this book was not a labour of love of sorts. Only someone who is a naturally loving and caring person would take the time to pen such a moving yet intrinsically helpful book. In no way was it a mindless, uninspired collection of strung-together words. Kelly Markey has once again proven why she has earned the title of bestselling author, which, in my opinion, is not a title to be taken lightly - especially if I'm going by traditional standards.

One of the noteworthy elements of this book is that Kelly produced a wealth of thought-provoking opportunities for readers. It is something that would be greatly appreciated by those with a strong inclination to personal development. Also, not to give away too much but the journal aspect, which lists pointed questions, also gently urges you to do a deep-dive with introspection.

As a qualified curator in the field of Image Management, which centres around personal and professional development, I almost felt as if this book can very well contribute to the holistic transformation of an individual. Also, an account of how her colleagues perceived her as she strutted into their universe in her power suit and sleek hairstyle stuck with me. Was it because I'm an Image Consultant? Maybe but I think it was because I fully understand the power of perception and personal branding. Kelly, in those moments, exuded charisma and confidence. Her personal ways would have then displayed her ethics and integrity.

As my eyes continued to grab greedily at the carefully crafted paragraphs, all I could hear myself say mentally was a whispered, "Wow." The rhetoric. The imagery created. The word and phrase selections. It was all a carefully written and tentful mastery of literature. There was always something that drew me deeper into the book and made me fixated on wondering what else she was going to expound on. From relationships to work trauma and wins to the rollercoaster, curveball events of life, Kelly found ways to churn out the silver lining or at the very least, hope of one.

Kelly's core essence in real life leans towards grace, class, humility, kindness, loyalty, quiet determination and peace. With her offering via this book, she was able to share her nature skilfully yet almost surreptitiously in various ways.

When the last page of the book has been read, it is without doubt that readers would have already had some profound and positive effect occur within their soul. In our lives, we are - or even have to be - multi-dimensional. We all have idiosyncrasies, flaws and faults but we should also be cognizant of, highlight and celebrate our beautifully imperfectly perfect selves, whilst yet ensuring that as the calendar pages are flipped, our personal inclinations are constantly evolving. Kelly gently clears the path for readers to accomplish just that and masterfully so.

I would say that she has once again successfully managed to create and add to her unique patches of the quilt of legacy in this life.

Nicole S. Farrell is a unique Image Consultant and Public Relations & Strategic Communications Strategist who has been in the Media industry in various capacities for over 20 years. She is an entrepreneur who is also a gifted multi-creative, two-time Author and dynamic International Speaker. Her portfolio includes being the Director for Communications on the Board of Directors within the Global Chamber of Business Leaders.

Preface

Are you modest enough to recognise that you are not superior to others and judicious enough to know that you are distinctly different? Refrain from waiting for life to meet your anticipations and start modifying your expectations to meet your life. If you carry one thing throughout your life, let it be courage. Let it be the courage to change the things that no longer serve you or humanity. Cultivate a life that acknowledges the bedlam of leaving a legacy – become the head honcho of your life! Your persona will dictate what remnants will remain long after you are gone. Necessitate a herculean effort to leave something worthy. The most important thing we extract from the earth is our existence… mother Earth nourishes you in profound ways… leave something tasteful before you depart "Please think about your legacy because you are writing it every day." – Gary Vaynerchuk.

I watched a documentary on the mastermind behind the construction of Machu Picchu. It is constructed in a terrain that is almost impossible to build. It exhibits a dominant blueprint to supply water, protection from the elements, and a carefully designed and fortified entrance that will require minimal resources to protect the fort should the need arise. This treasure had been hidden for over four centuries, even from the ordinary Inca people. This history engrossed me at this marvel and how deliberate these people were even in ancient times. A precise and divisive plan was created and remains a testimony that can never fade from history.

A durable hypothesis unravelled in my mind that my life is no different in so many parallels. As I embarked on this journey from a young bud to a blossomed woman, I was handed cards that depicted the terrain as unfavourable to build anything. However, life allowed me to decrypt my mind; if anything, substantial is worthy of construction: It takes time, sweat, blood, tears, death, purging, isolation, resources, perseverance, grit, willpower, and a tad more than elbow grease. Part of my story is captured in my book 'Don't Just Fly, SOAR' – even the book cannot capture all the precision that brought me to this point. And thus, I will not attempt to unravel it here.

Some days I could not see fine, even with the binoculars. We all know better, but do we do better? Even in ancient times, the Incas planned and designed with a target vision. We live in a time when we have all the modern conveniences, yet we rarely live by a definitive plan. I popped into the world with no plan. Growing up in segregation was the assumed everyday landscape in Southern Africa, and it did not prepare me to travel, live, and work on international platforms. Living in segregation sheltered me from what others felt. Discrimination was modelled to me in such obtuse fashions outside the South African borders. I invite the world to look at my personal experience in my book.

I was just a kid when I discovered that my loved ones were not always around me to protect me in the heart of danger. I was fortified to believe I could only depend on myself, and I, as no human, could be my ever-present help in the most significant point of need. God showed me season after season that He will protect me and send the right people to my path at every point in my life to sustain, help, nurture, and challenge me. No one's life is void of trial. We are simply not growing if we are not challenged. I was confronted with all the significant catastrophes under the sun. The chorus of why I played its tune until I had to fight it back with tears and say why NOT me? I have what it takes to endure this, grow, and emerge the victor. And so I did, and before I could polish the metaphoric badge of victory and pin it onto my lapel, the next challenge arrived bright and early, waiting to be unravelled.

At that moment, everything changed. I decided that I would not be a victim of any circumstance. I resolved to always look at the opportunities and, more strategically, not to let the predicaments of life kill the promises of my life. It was shocking to discover that not every character in the universe plays by the same rules. Some have no rules, and others change the rules. It was the proudest day of my life; I couldn't stop smiling when I experienced firsthand that God vindicated me in His sweet time. I understood that everything has its learning curve, no matter how painful. The lesson is coupled with a blessing.

I was like a water droplet at the edge of a leaf waiting to fall into the expanse and disappear for centuries with no trace of my existence, somewhat like Machu Picchu. God, in His infinite wisdom, had a better plan. He found me in the height of my despair and spoke to me, and He continues to speak to me. He showed me how to survive, and just as the Incas had the wisdom to build a water system that sustained them in rugged terrain, God sustained me too. Rest assured that if He did it in ancient times and for me, He can sustain you too. You too can leave a legacy that can never fade from history.

This Legacy Playbook is a legacy planner that chronicles my experiences, the lessons gleaned, and a platform to ignite your thoughts. It will compel you to peel back layers and self-examine your life, goals, character, and what legacy you are consciously or unconsciously building. This legacy plan is an opportunity to perfectly fine-tune your life and future. Remember, if you target nothing, you are likely to achieve nothing. This opportunity will help you focus on creating a significant legacy while you prepare your character and destiny to draw closer to a paragon.

As documented in my bestselling book Don't Just Fly, SOAR, I talk about a season in life where you may feel dead like an inanimate piece of wood, but life and hope can still sprout. Here is the excerpt from my book. "Numbers 17:8 – The next day, when Moses went into the tent, flowers and almonds were already growing on Aron's stick. This scripture reminds me of how I felt like a dead piece of wood, and then the spirit touched me, and I sprouted to life just like this dead staff of Aaron's sprouted with almond buds when it was in the holy presence of God. If God can make a dead piece of wood bloom, then rest assured you and I have hope too. So often in life, as we navigate difficult circumstances, we lose our ability to see logically and look at the broader picture to make informed decisions for our greater welfare. We focus on the quick fix. We want what feels right for the moment, even when it does not correlate with logic and reason. There is no instant fix in life as everything is a process."

Find the process that helps you to align. This book is a practical workbook to assist you with your alignment. Goals + Character Building = LEGACY PLAYBOOK. This is a navigated path to discover who you are and what you want to unleash. The sophistication of society is delicately and boldly poised by the freedom to choose. You have the basic rights to choose most things in your life. What is manifesting in your life? Unconventional to the end... exceptional about what? Growth will demand change. Are you ready to rumble with it? Are you a character that never allows accuracy to get in the way of truth... what can you smell apart from the lack of glory? In the gladiatorial fight of death, do not let the play of life elude you! Do not live your life drifting like a dead piece of wood. You are designed for more. "The great use of life is to spend it for something that will outlast it." – William James.

Do not drift like a dead piece of wood. Sprout somthing in your life.

How To Use and Benefit from This Playbook

I wrote this book to offer both inspiration and self-help with ample opportunities for self-examination within these pages. This book is informed by personal experience, historical case studies, and research. Each story is written to encourage self-awareness and critical thinking. You can use this book in any format that suits you: reading and journaling at your own pace, with your spouse, an accountability buddy, connect group, team building, or online sessions with a larger network.

Each chapter contains self-help prompts to guide you to unravel where and how you prefer to develop. This section may require you to think deeply and have significant conversations with yourself or others.

- ♦ Create a plan to review your growth

- ♦ Evaluate your development

- ♦ Develop an action plan

- ♦ Seek feedback regarding your development

- ♦ This voyage will create awareness of your eternal footprint

- ♦ This expedition will assist you to craft a lasting legacy

If you require granular details to create a vision, action steps, and assess risks, you can find a comprehensive list of 25 self-help tools in my book *Don't Just Fly, SOAR* to assist you.

Once you have completed each self-help section in this book:

- ♦ You will feel accomplished with your goal of creating a legacy.

- ♦ You may need more guidance from your network or a professional to assist you.

- ♦ Contact the author directly to engage in personal coaching sessions   @kellymakey.com

Finding Opportunities Where the World Sees Obstacles

During my sojourn to San Francisco, I cruised the shoreline dotted with seals. As the noontide sun glistened with The Golden Gate Bridge behind me and the wind sweeping my hair in every direction. I braced the bad hair moment and marinated in the enticing reality. The epic backdrop! The historical foreground is what dreams are made of.

Then pondering the essence of this tourist hot spot. One of the attractions that hijacked my attention – Alcatraz Prison, often called 'The Rock.' During the age of 1930s prohibition, many famous gangsters and criminals were housed there, most notably Al Capone and Machine Gun Kelly. During its entire history, no prisoner managed to escape Alcatraz successfully. In 14 escape attempts, 36 prisoners tried to escape, and 23 were caught. Eight died on the run, and five remaining are missing and drowned. Inmates Frank Morris, John Anglin, and Clarence Anglin managed to exit the prison complex walls and enter the icy waters of San Francisco Bay. Their bodies were never found, and although the officials claim they most certainly drowned, the U.S. Marshall Office is still investigating this case.

Nicknamed 'The Rock,' it did live up to its reputation. So, what gave these men the remote possibility to venture outside the square and think they could escape and live to tell the tale? Many factors may contribute to their curated plans. I simply zoomed in as an engrossed tourist to note that a few men saw an opportunity where no opportunity existed. All efforts spelled nothing but demise, yet they took the plunge. Granted motivation kicks us all with zeal, and imprisonment may do that. But for those not incarcerated, do we hone into an opportunity where the world has planted nothing but obstacles?

Are we conditioned by a culture to always profess defeat to anything that requires elbow grease and proactive planning? Do we sprinkle our lives with a negative dust of deceit from the onset by making negative remarks? *'This is too hard,'* '*I don't have the time,'* and '*I don't have the money, skills, or talent to do this.*' Wake up your instinct to be rational and look for the opportunity to find a solution. Steel yourself from first impressions. Learn to evaluate the threats and consequences objectively. Learn to identify and resolve real problems. Master the art to swift out exaggerated imaginary issues. Build your internal hide to ignore reactions and focus on improvements.

Obstacles are packaged as physical, mental, emotional, cultural, or global constraints – limiting but not impossible to conquer. Every barrier provides a learning curve and a rich experience. Looking for opportunities begins with your mindset. Seek the lesson from every curve ball and use it to build your cathedral of victory. You need a strategy with a realistic roadmap. Expect problems – things go wrong, and people will let us down. Zoom in on solutions and improvements rather than grumbling around the same mountain. Cultivate inner fortitude and discernment. Evaluate every predicament or opportunity and give it realistic context. Build muscles to endure hardships and grow. Let wisdom guide you with finesse to take charge and control, or simply walk away. Become competent to discover the art of losing the battle with grace to win the war with honour.

The solution is always in your hands. Setbacks are just stepping stones for a comeback to carve your next leap forward. Ultimately you are in control of all the possibilities, and the circumstances don't dictate your direction. Unfair conditions simply reveal the grit you are composed of to sink or soar. Authentic characters will not let changing obstacles direct their lives. Define your goal and resolve to attain it regardless of the obstacle course that spins you upside down.

Failure teaches us how to analyse, remediate, and retry. So never shy away from gaining a stripe of experience that will one day transcend to excellence. Tackle every obstacle with zeal, and you may achieve what's branded as the *'impossible,'* leaving the whole world wondering how you found the pluck to break that rock. The possibilities are endless.

Fear speaks of what if, faith declares EVEN IF – know the difference. Have you ever seen a weed finding a tiny gap in a crack in a concrete floor and growing, blooming, and flourishing like someone planted it there on purpose and rendered it with a healthy dose of tender loving care? It's an image to me that captions, EVEN IF YOU POUR CONCRETE OVER MY HABITAT, I WILL FLOURISH.

The concept of hope sounds static, but it is, in fact, dynamic. Both you and I can find that tiny hairline crack of hope in every situation to push our way above and beyond. Do not conform to the rigid taboo of giving up based on the presented harsh circumstances. Resolve to offer your life the hypothesis which has intrinsic merit to create something beautiful from the scraps that steal your tears. Be a creator. It's easy to create when you have the resources; however, the merit is framed when you create something significant out of the dregs. Relish the amalgam of experience, opportunity, and knowledge to be a master builder. Develop your destiny. When it is the season of lemons, then make lemonade.

You don't have to wait a decade for the humiliation to disappear. Absorb the influence of the current state then, no matter how harsh it may seem, dig up your confidence and zeal one day or hour at a time. Eventually, the shame topples off instantly, then practice for your behaviour to catch up! *'The art of knowing is to know what to ignore'* – Rumi. Seen and unseen disease enfeebles both our mind and body, so create a path to find your focus. Find something to guide you from the dark season to a better tomorrow. Laugh in the places you cried, change the narrative, and re-write history while transitioning your conscience.

There are millions of goal-slayers in this world. They have climbed the ladder to success and found meagre fulfilment at the summit. Cultivate the path with your mental leap. Attach your self-worth to your net worth. Strategically be aware of what gives you your net worth. You will march to that beat and live it out loud when you know your core values. The riddle of life is tantalising, but that gets lost when you don't understand your values and what you can and cannot do. When you don't know your limit and direction, others influence you to sing the song that rocks their world. You slowly lose the essence of yourself.

The seeds of a miracle are frequently planted in the soil of an unpleasant situation. There is vast opportunity in every circumstance. It comes to life when you begin the act of deliberate – not accidental – effort. What you bond with, you become bound to. Do not be a prisoner in the life of your lies; don't spend your entire life honouring other people's expectations of you. Break free, and live your zeal out loud. Forge a life that makes no apology for its opulence. A character is a class act. Grow the enthusiasm to flourish even where others see no opportunity. Refrain from allowing your ego to bind you to be loyal to your mistakes. Never live in a prison of your problems. Only you can break free. Men even escaped from 'The Rock', so what's holding you back?

You are not living your best life because you are surviving your old life. The pain of walking into the unfamiliar may stifle you, but millions of old and young, rich and poor people take risks every day. Risks benefit their experience and growth. Alacrity is still active and passionately alive, so take the plunge. Dive in and tame that beast to your tone. You may have received corrupt indoctrination in apprenticeship days, but now is the time to shake it off like the snake sheds its skin and leap into something new. You don't have to live with that old thing created for you.

Sometimes, our wants may be irrelevant, but what is evident is what ticks all the etiquette boxes to forge to the next level – a new and enhanced you rising out of a bad situation like a phoenix stronger than ever. What made you cry yesterday will give you strength next week. Forge ahead if you want to do something. You will find a way. If you don't, you will find an excuse. Awaken the fake up. We are suffocating in an influx of information while the deficiencies of wisdom starve in startling styles. What do you starve in your life, and what you feed will define how you find opportunities in the forest of obstacles?

We degenerate rapidly to points where we are haunted by memories that we were too afraid to re-engineer or plan then sudden siege compels us to introspect. Grow from the vision in the mirror as well. Graduate from your barren decisions and become pregnant with finer choices that will feed future generations and alter the tides of fate. *'Every storm runs out of rain.'* – Maya

Angelou. Outlive that storm… rise and grab your territory of opportunity to make a difference, no matter how minor or significant.

Tragically, even when some people have an advantage, they only zoom into the obstacle. How do you tackle obstacles?

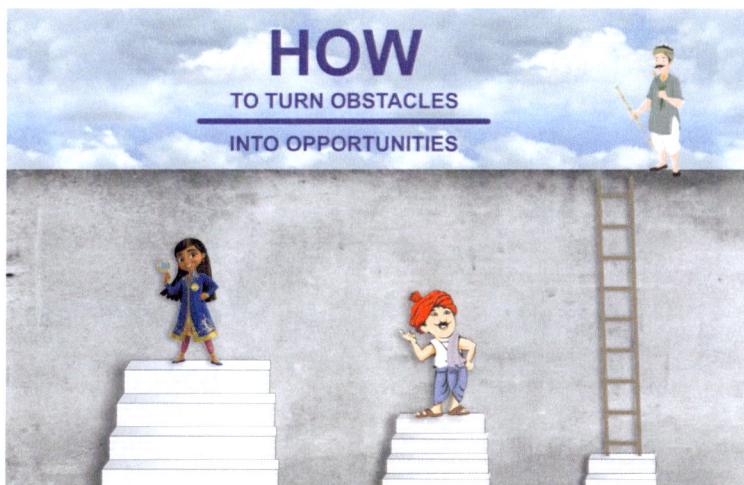

Creating Your Legacy

"If you would not be forgotten as soon as you are dead, either write something worth reading or do something worth writing." — Benjamin Franklin

Have you evaluated the barren parts of your life?

_____
_____
_____
_____

Did anyone ever tell you that you cannot do something, and did you prove them wrong?

_____
_____
_____
_____

What is your greatest victory, and how has this impacted humanity?

_____
_____
_____
_____

What are your grateful for?

_____
_____
_____
_____

Do you align your words with your actions daily?

_____
_____
_____
_____
_____

Personal Development Goals

_____
_____
_____
_____
_____
_____
_____
_____
_____
_____
_____
_____
_____
_____
_____
_____
_____
_____
_____
_____
_____
_____
_____
_____
_____
_____
_____
_____
_____
_____
_____
_____

Don't Just Fly But Soar in Relationships

Comprehend that if life is dandy for you, that is not the same for everyone else. Learn to be a friend if your confidence comes with a cherry on top. Develop the art of caring and discard resentment. When strategically avoiding that challenging conversation, you craft a perceived quick win masked with prolonged dysfunction. The global divorce statistics are staggering. What's contributing to this equation of despair? So many shattered lives, dreams, and a generation of scars... strands in the cord of truth! Moving to the tyranny of urgency requires us all to march to the beat of change, an amendment from the cycle defined by data to be doomed truly before the romance has blossomed. Idolatry is well and truly alive in our plans to dream the dream but give up once the gloom is forecasted. We run for the hills without profound effort. A sedentary culture is churning along.

A curated community never greatly pressed for want of pity, so we move on swiftly to the next unsuspecting best thing. Your acrimony habituates to a kernel of loathing. Why not adopt a proactive approach and go in with your eyes wide open to avoid contributing to the statistics? Love brings our broken bits together and keeps us close when we tell each other our secrets. The beast of mistrust is not the path to remain stuck in. Life also offers us rich relationships in other facets outside the romantic boat. The same basic skills are required to flourish and soar in any **REAL**ationship. Be aware of all the forces at play and decorate your stress away one meaningful interaction at a time. Create positive vibes on purpose, no matter how difficult the situation is. Look for the silver lining every time.

Do you **not** allow new people to love you since people hurt you in the past? Have you left the baggage at the door? A dime a dozen think they have, but so much drama manifests at the most inopportune time just because we lack the skills to tackle the elephant in the room and heal. You cannot annoy my anchored soul, so before you leap into anything: marriage, friendship, partnership, leadership, volunteer, or work team member, understand what anchors you. How deep are your roots? Will you survive a storm? Do you simply avoid any signs of a storm like the plague and buckle in? Your senses for people will alter drastically as you acquire knowledge to love yourself, understand your core values, and not make compromises that will taint your world.

'Self-Love, a.k.a. my rights' proudly emblazoned on every platform and so many lips. There is much to declare for having a healthy level of self-worth and exercising appropriate self-care. The scriptures do not share our preoccupation with self. Consider, for example, Jesus' famous words in Luke 9:23, *'Whoever wants to be my disciple must deny themselves and take up their cross daily and follow me.'* This enlightens us to focus on others instead of constantly zooming in on our personal needs. Piled misjudgement on misfortune is the result when we are constantly self-seeking. Break the mould and celebrate the other party. It will propel you into a new season. We are essentially in a facet of relationship 24/7, so develop both the awareness and skills to soar at it.

Commitment, responsibility, and honesty propel us to create sparks and rapport in the bedroom, boardroom, or any social platform. Has all traces of blame and victimhood left the building? Positive relations embody presence that is tendered and manicured daily – it is purposeful. Thriving networks communicate about anything and everything. It is courageous, vulnerable, and loyal, with no smokescreens or secrets. You cannot plan for the future unless you properly address the past in all associations. Consider the tone in which you speak. Extend gently with your experience. In addition, develop the art of offering your undivided attention as depicted by Richard Moss *'The greatest gift you can give another is the purity of your attention.'* Don't use primitive smoke code to communicate. Use jargon-free language to reach your audience, even if you do not use verbatim. A wise woman understands the precise psychological moment when to say nothing yet say so much with no words, artful tact at its pinnacle best. *'There are some people who could hear you speak a thousand words and still not understand you. There are others who will understand you – without you even speaking a word.'* Yasmin Mogahed. Unconditional love distinctly differs from unconditional tolerance... know the difference – the subject of knowledgeable arguments if you have to partake.

The greatest litmus test is how you handle the relationship when it plummets down south, where the twists and turns take you – do you lose the plot? Do you become bitter or better? What lessons do you glean from the ending season? The intricate facets also include establishing and maintaining your boundaries, respecting boundaries from others, unlearning bad habits, and teaching yourself new things to add value to the new escarpment of fellowship.

There is ample de**LIGHT** in harnessing an authentic relationship with yourself. A milestone where you have plateaued to be comfortable in your skin, and there is no prerequisite for others to rush in and validate your existence like quartz clockwork. Delightfully sardonic tweetup throws some relationships in the spotlight. A love story that captured hearts worldwide when Meghan Markle and Prince Harry shared matrimony bliss. Their fairy tale has been untraditional, yet it tarries. The love shared between the couple continues to conquer the mammoth trials. One curve ball after the next, vast hullabaloo, but they are still smiling and making those vows work. Everyone has a path that will stretch and bend them, but we need to find our focus to ride on what boosts us. No characterised cultural soirée is completed without grit. Find your perseverance switch. Do you have the grit to transcend from sand to glass?

Craving any emotional connection in authentic conversations is a sure tell-tale that you have deficiencies. Develop self-awareness for these red flags so you do not bond to someone unhealthy to satisfy your needs. Have that difficult conversation with your significant other and create a way to debar uninvited intrusion. Never apologise for burning too brightly. Let your zeal shine; if it bothers others, consider the reasons objectively. Why are people jealous or intimidated? May your choices demonstrate your ordered hopes and not reflect your brewing phobias. When you judge me without knowing me, you do not define me. You describe yourself, so let people paint themselves while you live your best life with those that fundamentally matter. Park the noise in the dark corner. Information brings revelation, and revelation ignites transformation.

It is not your responsibility to heal others. However, it is your obligation to reconcile the fragments of you that resonate with their brokenness. Manipulation is when people blame you for your reaction to their disrespect. We compose a story expressing how to intermingle with us now and in the future! Sometimes we have to make a decision that will hurt our hearts but will heal our souls. Align your values to reach your North Star, instead of avoiding the elephant in the room yet again – grab it by the tusk and tame it.

Practicing gratitude doesn't entail concealing unwelcome emotions or seeking the silver lining in an adverse condition. Committed appreciation means acknowledging what is quite decent along with the disarray. Fling away the notion that you must pause your life until you are fundamentally healed. Make wholesome choices for your present and future within the pain... that's where victory steps in and takes charge to change the narrative. Remember, you are always responsible for how you act, no matter how you feel.

Healing yourself can be offensive to people that benefit from your brokenness. When you begin to restore, develop, revolutionise, and transcend, it does shift the dynamics in our social vortex, some drift away, but real friends will celebrate the new layers of your success. The best revenge is investing in yourself and creating a prosperous future.

Normal is a setting on a washing machine and not a status to dictate life. No relationship is normal. Each one has its uniqueness and significance. The measure of a good man is to plant a tree under which he is acutely aware he will never sit in the shade it spreads. Yet the gesture banquets a lingering quench to something in muted tones that speak louder than the gesture itself. What a splendid act of giving with no demand to be repaid for the good deed. Envision what all the relationships would be like if we all adopted the passion for giving without any expectations. Give your time, energy, resources, and love to others with the comfort of knowing it is well with your soul, even if they don't appreciate you. Focus on your journey, the seeds you plant on the way, and the lives you impact now and in the future. The greatest sin is unconscious, and considerable sadness is when humans refuse to remove the blindfold. There's hope that calls out courage. Let it manifest in you. Focus on what you dish out to the world, and all your relationships will align.

Creating Your Legacy

"Immortality is to live your life doing good things, and leaving your mark behind." — Brandon Lee

What major lesson has your relationship revealed to you?

_____
_____
_____
_____

What are you gleaning, restoring from, maturing about, and ascertaining about yourself and your significant other?

_____
_____
_____
_____

How have you advanced in the last six months, year, and since the relationship?

_____
_____
_____
_____

What facet of the relationship are you most grateful for, communication, sex, friendship, soulmate, chemistry, physical attraction, unconditional love, or security?

_____
_____
_____
_____

What is your favourite habit with your partner, and why is this routine important to you?

_____
_____
_____
_____

Personal Development Goals

Resilience

Off the coast of Italy, a volcanic eruption many years ago, now show life despite the harmful gases, bacteria, fish, sea plants, and a whole ecosystem exists. Nature has a way of bringing forth life after the devastation, resilience at its best.

In July 2020, we had our wedding plans to say *'I do'* in Santorini, the Greek Island dream stolen from us due to the COVID-19 pandemic. We spent the first three years of marriage in the confines of this global pandemic. International border closures, lockdowns, numerous virus variants, and balancing working from home. We all needed that resilience pill overdose that season. Courtesy of Wikipedia: *'Psychological resilience is the ability to mentally or emotionally cope with a crisis or to return to pre-crisis status quickly. Resilience exists when the person uses mental processes and behaviours in promoting personal assets and protecting self from the potential negative effects of stressors.'*

So eloquently described, but just how do we put this into practice? Life is complex, even without a pandemic in the whirlwind. A survey conducted by Everyday Health, in partnership with the Ohio State University, found that 83 percent of Americans believe they have high emotional and mental resilience levels. In reality, only 57 percent scored as resilient. Physical resilience refers to the body's ability to adapt to challenges and recover quickly. Community resilience refers to the ability of groups of people to respond to and recover from adverse situations, such as natural disasters, acts of violence, or economic hardship.

Despite having tools to predict our resilience levels, we are all wired differently, and a reflection in this hour may be incorrect later that same day. So, learn to gauge your internal vector. Being resilient does not mean that people don't experience tension, emotional commotion, and distress. Some people equate resilience with mental toughness, but demonstrating resilience includes working through emotional pain and suffering. Living out that demonstration is key. Resilience is not a status update, where you are on one moment and off the next. It's more like hiking a mountain without a trail map, and the conditions are against you. It takes focus, time, grit, and support from people around you, and you will most likely experience setbacks along the way. But eventually, you reach the top and look back at how far you have come. Perseverance is the buzzword.

Resilience is vital because it gives people the forte to process and overcome adversity. Those lacking resilience are overwhelmed and may turn to unwholesome survival mechanisms. Resilient people tap into their strengths and support systems to overcome challenges and solve problems. Scientists have discovered sea slugs that sometimes detach their heads and regrow their entire bodies, according to a study published in the Current Biology journal. We know of many instances of this process, called *'autotomy,'* such as when lizards regrow their tails. It is suspected they use photosynthesis to survive while their organs are regrowing. Granted, we are a different species but we can absorb from this process. In the name of survival, let go of what does not serve you, use what you have to maintain yourself, and always grow something new. Life becomes much simpler when you let people misunderstand you, and circumstances underestimate you – concentrate on what edifies your soul. Come out of several rodeos with ample experience and skills to charter through high water and the resilience badge.

Commit to forge fortresses from the fragments of your fellowship and friendships. Create the resolution to never hit these two buttons by default: panic and snooze at any season in life. As slow as the slug is, he is re-growing its body. Stay focused on the goal – even if you are moving at a slug pace. You are moving, and that's all that matters. Rise each morning, making a small step closer to your goal.

The 7 Cs resilience model was developed by paediatrician Ken Ginsberg, MD, to help children and adolescents build resilience. *Learning competence, confidence, connection, character, contribution, coping, and control* is how Ginsberg says we can build inner strength and utilize outside resources — regardless of age. Use this as your foundation building to create your powerhouse of resilience. Look to those who walked before you and glean from their life and lessons how you can better equip yourself to wear the fragrance of resilience.

"Deeply hurt by the death of her mother, thirty-five-year-old Agatha Christie was still trying to overcome her grief when her husband of twelve years suddenly announced that he was in love with another woman and wanted a divorce. The twin shocks threw Agatha into a deep state of depression. Feeling that the best of life was behind her, she saw little reason to go on living. Only concern for her seven-year-old daughter saved her from suicide. In time Agatha began to recover from the pain of her failed marriage. She resumed writing and, to boost her spirits, took a trip on the Orient Express. Then, in 1930 a friend invited her to come along on a trip to an archaeological dig in Iraq. There she met Max Mallowan, a prominent archaeologist thirteen years her junior. They fell in love and were married later that year, a happy marriage that would last until Agatha's death 46 years later.

At the end of 1926, Agatha Christie may have thought that her life was no longer worth living, but she was entirely wrong about that. In the years that followed, she not only found the love of her life, but she also enjoyed her greatest success, becoming the best-loved author on earth, with over 70 best-selling novels as well as the longest-running play in history. Her husband Max was knighted in 1968, and three years later Agatha was made a Dame of the British Empire. Agatha Mary Clarissa Miller Christie Mallowan died at age 85 on January 12, 1976. With over two billion copies sold, she is the best-selling novelist in history."

What takes a person from suicidal to a bestselling author in history? The most prominent thing is **RESILIENCE**. People face all kinds of adversity in life. Personal crises include illness, loss of a loved one, abuse, bullying, job loss, divorce, miscarriage, and financial instability. There is the shared reality of tragic events in the news, such as terrorist attacks, mass shootings, natural disasters, and the COVID-19 pandemic. People must learn to cope with and work through challenging life experiences. Life may not come with a map, but everyone will experience twists and turns, from everyday challenges to traumatic events with more lasting impacts, like the death of a loved one, a life-altering accident, or a serious illness. Each change affects people differently, bringing a unique flood of thoughts, potent emotions, and uncertainty. Yet people generally adapt well over time to life-changing and stressful situations, partly thanks to resilience.

Like building anything of value, growing your resilience takes time and intention. Psychologists have identified some factors that appear to make a person more resilient, such as a positive attitude, optimism, the ability to regulate emotions, and the ability to see failure as a form of helpful feedback. Optimism, for instance, has been shown to help blunt the impact of stress on the mind and body in the wake of disturbing experiences. That gives people access to their cognitive resources, enabling cool-headed analysis of what might have gone wrong and consideration of behavioural paths that might be more productive. Other aspects of resilience's roots appear to be a genetic predisposition. For instance, early environments and life circumstances affect how resilient genes are ultimately expressed.

Does trauma make someone less resilient? Not necessarily. People who have undergone trauma can often be highly resilient. I shared the traumas and comebacks that life dished out to me in my book: *'Don't Just Fly, SOAR.'* This is a testimony to my resilience and confirmation that we do not have to let trauma derail us. Get back up on the horse and try once more. Many factors determine resilience, such as genetics, early life experiences, and sheer fluke. These components cannot be modified. But specific resilience-building skills can be learned. These include breaking out negative thought cycles, pushing back against catastrophizing, and looking for the positive in each setback. Seeking help from a licensed professional.

It will leave a stain on your soul – the circle of life. Triumph through discomfort and disillusionment is not essentially easy for anyone to navigate. Researchers have uncovered what more resilient people do to emotionally and mentally carry on after the death of a loved one, a job loss, chronic or acute illness, or another obstacle. Which cohort do you identify with? Do you demand a perfect streak, or can you accept that life is a mix of losses and wins? In each case, the latter quality has been tied to greater resilience. In addition, healthy habits are paramount to resilience: getting enough sleep, eating well, and exercising. All these practices can reduce stress, which may, in turn, enhance resilience. Equally, cultivating significant relationships can help an individual find support when a catastrophe arises. Frequently thinking about morals and actively living according to one's values have been linked to higher resilience. We can all weather that storm one drop at a time.

Your mindset is correlated too how resilient you are. Ascertain areas of irrational thinking and align yourself to focus on the positive rather than the gloomy. Perhaps you cannot change an extremely stressful event, but you can change how you interpret and respond to it. Also, make peace with reality and accept that change is a part of life. A confident attitude enables you to expect good things. Along the way, maintain an audit log of any subtle ways you start to feel better. Then strategically follow your pattern. Learn from your past. By looking back at who or what was helpful in previous times of distress, you may discover how to respond effectively to new difficult situations. Go light up the world as you bounce back.

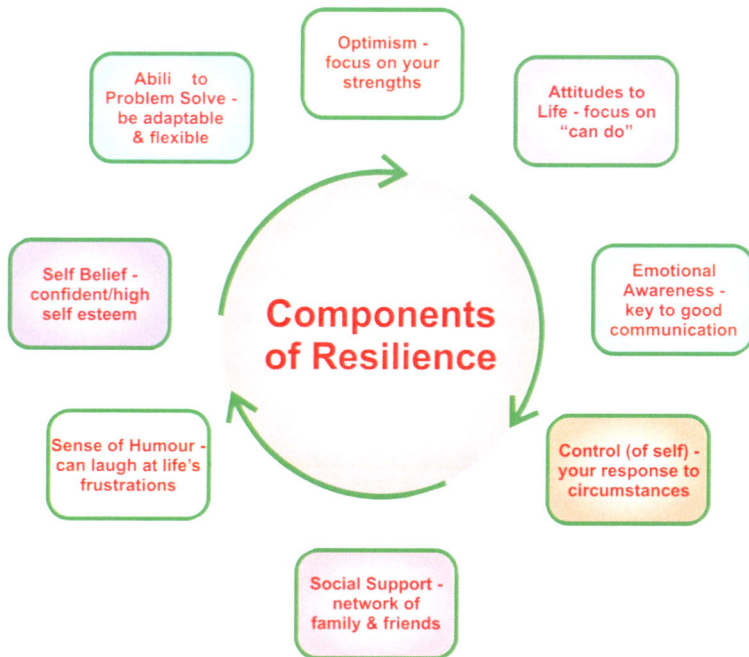

Optimism - focus on your strengths

Abili to Problem Solve - be adaptable & flexible

Attitudes to Life - focus on "can do"

Self Belief - confident/high self esteem

Components of Resilience

Emotional Awareness - key to good communication

Sense of Humour - can laugh at life's frustrations

Control (of self) - your response to circumstances

Social Support - network of family & friends

Creating Your Legacy

"Our days are numbered. One of the primary goals in our lives should be to prepare for our last day. The legacy we leave is not just in our possessions, but in the quality of our lives. What preparations should we be making now? The greatest waste in all of our earth, which cannot be recycled or reclaimed, is our waste of the time that God has given us each day." — Bill Graham

Describe your favourite source of rest.

_____

_____

_____

_____

How do you unwind daily and annually?

_____

_____

_____

_____

Do you know when you have reached burnout?

_____

_____

_____

_____

Explain the recent event where you displayed resilience.

_____

_____

_____

_____

Define something that you do for yourself daily to prioritise your self-care.

_____

_____

_____

Personal Development Goals

_____

_____

_____

_____

_____

_____

_____

_____

_____

_____

_____

_____

_____

_____

_____

_____

_____

_____

_____

_____

_____

_____

_____

_____

_____

_____

_____

_____

_____

_____

_____

_____

Confidence

Camaraderie with fair authority and authentic twinkle of perseverance breeds CONFIDENCE in many untold ways. It fashions a path of an unquestionably durable allure in the landscape on both the corporate and personal facets. We forge forward, trying to quell the colour rising in our cheeks as we project real or perceived confidence. The lexicon derivative is: *'Confidence means feeling sure of yourself and your abilities – not in an arrogant way, but in a realistic and secure way.'*

Typical exemplars are trust, commitment, self-assurance, and keeping a lid on something told in secret. Confidence is a fusion of esteem and efficacy and many things in-between. Let's turn our focus to what confidence is not: It most definitely does not believe in the illusion of perfection and the drumbeat to conform to perfectionism as a character standard. It is not the impression that life is free from trials and tribulations. It is most certainly not unrealistic expectations set by others or oneself. It is not a license to be self-serving. The lack of confidence will create a whirlwind that may trap you with self-doubt, worthlessness, an inferiority complex, apathy, anxiety, depression, and the list goes on.

It is crucial to understand what self-confidence is and the reality of accepting your faults and foibles. Standing tall regardless, while you act vigorously because you believe in your inherent worth and value. It is so vital that we understand what confidence brings to the table: awareness and limitations and how to balance your life with both. Realization and acceptance of what's possible, desired, wanted, and coveted – get a realistic snapshot. Reaching contentment. The potential to create an authentic experience and craft happiness into your life.

If a camel is a horse designed by a committee, then how will society calculate confidence? I sojourned to New York, to celebrate my 40th birthday. At breakfast, my friend played a video created by my friends in Sydney – all beautiful birthday wishes. One of my male friends, in the video, went on to describe... *'Kelly, you made a real impression on us all, waltzing in with your white corporate suit and hair all slicked black – like a woman with real purpose and seeping so much CONFIDENCE.'* Then a few days later, my friend that played the video in New York went on to tease me about this line. I caught myself introspecting myself, to discover the contours of my character! A resolute personality rises to the challenge – grandstand for the fiercest competition to evaluate who we truly are versus the perception of others.

Refrain from stagnating in your bubble of perceived perceptions, get into the real world, and test society's theory and the thread of every fibre that stacks up to define your confidence. I was born in the great escarpments of Southern Africa, where apartheid reigned. I grew up in a segregated community that was enforced by segregation bylaws. In essence, this environment was a default habitat, and it was all that I was exposed to. I attended school, lived, and shopped within the boundaries defined for my Indian demographics. We all lived in the very same bubble. We respected and cheered each other on as one joyful race.

My first employment was in South Africa for the federal government, and the taste and smell of division was oh so rife. The standard and expectations were almost set in stone, it only dictated compliance in every domain. Find your lane and stay there; this was subconsciously indoctrinated in me. Then I immigrated to New Zealand and eventually relocated to Australia. It came with a host of new challenges, but for the purpose of this article, I will zoom in on just one facet, my confidence. I was freshly shipped from a developing world that modelled nothing but apartheid to me! Suddenly I was thrust into a new environment – a cosmopolitan vortex. This new world spoke of equality and freedom, but many undercurrents were presented. The muted tones and string pulling were no different to find your lane and stay there.

I had to get up each morning and find my own internal moral compass, my self-esteem, my self-efficacy, and ultimately my self-confidence. I gleaned that my confidence came in small dollops in the little things I did and in the profound ways I stood up for my values, principles, and work ethics. My confidence was constructed in the manner I presented myself and the rooms I walked out off when my welfare was not served as the main course. With the progression of time, I can now walk into a room and watch the molecules move, simply because my confidence sets the tone. It's a learned skill – we are most definitely not born with it.

In essence, know your worth and what you bring to the table, understand your limitations, and be true to your values, and your confidence will find its way to you and take over the narrative like it is in your core DNA. The unaltered nomenclature of processing fame or status in small intellects is not the vibe of confidence. Confidence brings out the best in you for the best reasons. Everyone wants to knock the top dog off the step, but happy to see you be the underdog fighting for it. When you are confident in your own skin then you will not be inclined to knock anyone off their game or even dictate to others to remain in a labelled path. Real confidence is not just striving to live up to your worth but recognising that others around you have worth too, and you are not threatened by any other levels of confidence in the room.

The epic life of Harriet Tubman gives life to the meaning of confidence on steroids. I recall watching the movie about her life and was in awe. She had confidence in herself and had the zeal to inject her confidence into others, but most aptly, she used her confidence for the greater good, to help others to freedom. She did not settle for the crumbs thrown her way. She dug deep to bring up her confidence in truckloads. She did not even lack confidence when her own husband could not wait for her and took to another woman. Yes, indeed, she was hurt, but her confidence surged. She had the acumen to separate her pain and not allow it to derail her confidence. She was born a slave, and most around her complied with the dictated rules. Harriet Tubman was a fine woman of distinction; her self-confidence gave her the fragrant savour to freedom. She honed in on her talents and granted freedom to another 750 enslaved African-Americans – the sweeter taste of sovereignty. She understood the limitations around her, the community, and the laws of the land, yet her confidence prevailed.

Not all of us are born with confidence, it can be a real struggle for some of us. Life experience sometimes sends us into a cocoon and keeps us in a pattern of perpetual despair. Every tiny or gigantic step can help you leap out of that shell. Create a self-analysis of all the things you got right in your life and how you positively impacted others. Hone into your strengths and practice excelling in this facet of life. Define some micro and macro goals and plan to achieve them. Enhance your self-awareness, practice objective thinking, and listen actively when people offer advice – especially to correct and grow yourself. Strive to reduce negative thought patterns, learn skills to cope under pressure, don't be afraid to get things wrong, and don't wait for opportunities to come to you on a platter with your name etched in gold. While you are still in the pig pen, create new opportunities even when the whole world seems shut. Harriet found a way in the grimmest circumstances. Understand what the journey will cost you, know what you need to weather the storm, and find what you need to bounce back. Every setback must have come back to mature your confidence.

As soon as we act confident, we are already pretending – let the zeal ignite within. Live and breathe it with courage and conviction. Confidence is your North Star; you will be lost without it, and most around you will notice that at the onset. So, plan for your success, as confidence amplifies the trait of triumph. Confidence also paves the way to leadership if you want to write yourself into the script of leadership, polish up your confidence. Confidence presents hand in glove with substance – refrain from the shallow strut. It will not pay dividends. Non-verbal communication unlocks your confidence even before you unleash your verbatim – your body language reflects and reinforces confidence in a palatable fashion. Your vocal tone sets the scene – speak in statements, not questions, while you own the authority. Dress up with authentic vulnerability and genuineness, transcending typical uncertainty into substantiated confidence. Realise that, like everything of value, some elbow grease is required, and there is no magic wand; you must prepare to shed layers and grow – commit to a process. Realise that the philosophy *'fake it until you make it'* is a train wreck for confidence. Don't engage in people-pleasing behaviour, and stop comparing yourself. You need to run your own race; it's not a competition with others. Don't live in a prison of your limitations. You are not living your best life because you are surviving with your lingering failures. Setbacks are learning curves to launch forward.

Taking a scenic journey, life has so many twists and turns, and turning around one definitive corner is understanding that our confidence does not originate from society hammering the like button on social media. Despite many false correlations of people having their worth, value, and confidence tied up in the number of *'LIKES'* they accrue or fail to accumulate. This is not tethered to confidence. Healing is a quiet homecoming; it's about tracing the way back to yourself. Zooming out of the brokenness and focusing on your wholesome beauty. Seek to define your confidence, and don't rely on society to mirror it to you. If you are wrong, educate yourself, and don't let society belittle or degrade you. If you have made a mistake, communicate effectively, and gain clarity and support so that you may be receptive and open to wise words and communication in your life for you to change for the better and greater good – adding a rich layer of confidence to your weathered hide.

Robust people also have frail stints. Don't let your weak moments define your confidence level and, eventually, your charisma. Be strategic and know when and why to pause. *"Life is not easy for any of us. But what of that? We must have perseverance and, above all, confidence in ourselves. We must believe that we are gifted for something and that this thing must be attained."* – Marie Curie

Creating Your Legacy

"The little bit you and me might change the world," Malloy smiled, "it wouldn't show up until a hundred years after we were dead. We'd never see it. But it'd be there." — James Jones, From Here to Eternity

How do you unleash your confidence?

_____
_____
_____
_____

In what ways do you enhance your confidence?

_____
_____
_____
_____

What is your confidence tied up to?

_____
_____
_____
_____

How do you persevere when you are feeling low?

_____
_____
_____
_____

What makes you feel energized?

_____
_____
_____
_____
_____

Personal Development Goals

_____
_____
_____
_____
_____
_____
_____
_____
_____
_____
_____
_____
_____
_____
_____
_____
_____
_____
_____
_____
_____
_____
_____
_____
_____
_____
_____
_____
_____
_____

Negative Self Talk

Negative self-talk can take many forms. Constantly questioning if you are worthy or good enough, do you stack up? What is the ultimate benchmark to measure your voids? It may present a realistic appraisal of a situation, but what are you trying to measure here – yourself or how you stack up against your landscape? The spirit of asserting confidence and flaunting convention comes naturally for some, with no tertiary qualification required. This is the throes of life that torment us all when we invite negative self-talk to take a seat at the table. Life can get so busy that we navigate the path on autopilot and go about our day without noticing a single thought travelling through our minds. We all require a modicum of reflection to examine our conscious and unconscious thought patterns and how they colour our life.

Parallel to a rich, layered cake, our lives are conjured up with vast layers of history and a considerable storage system, it is mostly diminished at the edges by negative self-talk. The initial step to understanding negative self-talk is simply tuning in and starting to pay attention to our thoughts. The next step is challenging them. Self-talk is arguments, words, and expressions while thinking or talking to yourself. Sometimes self-talk can be helpful to keep us inspired toward goals. However, negative self-talk will sound more like an inner critic. What we do with our pain and choices contributes to our identity. If you drop dead today and an autopsy is done on you, where would you find negative self-talk in your body? Merit is found in knowing where it swells in your mind and how to deconstruct it.

Our negative self-talk, rather internal criticism, can be an all-encompassing manner we act based on what others spoke about us, our perceived lack of abilities. We hold on to the negative vibe society dispensed to us even when the landscape has changed. Scientifically our body rejuvenates. Scientists have unravelled that the body's cells largely replace themselves every 7 to 10 years. Essentially old cells mostly die and are replaced with new ones during this span. The cell renewal process happens more quickly in certain body parts, but head-to-toe rejuvenation can take up to a decade. Scientifically, we are a new creation every decade. Yet our mind remains stuck with so much from the past or who dished out what, where, and when. Technically our physical body is renewing itself to benefit us. We must now galvanise into action to make a material difference in replacing the internal dialogue. Don't have a new body with the stale old mind. Proactively work on renewing your negative self-talk as well.

Take an excursion into your consciousness. Catch yourself with your thoughts, self-introspect, watch your patterns, and be aware of your choices and how your negative self-talk hinders your outcomes in life. When I feel overwhelmed with a task, and my mind wants to drag me down a path, I focus on my North Star. My favourite scripture is *"I can do all things through Christ who strengthens me"* – Philippians 4:11–13. This launches me to shake off the negative self-talk and not permit it to derail me. I know that these musings are untrue, and I refuse to let them shape my life in any way, shape, or form. I shift my focus to words with positive valence. Create a habit of conducting constant mental merging akin to a filing system. We throw out what's unnecessary and file the important stuff for future use. Reward yourself and purge your mind in the same fashion. Negative self-talk limits your ability to believe in yourself and your ability to reach your potential. It is any thought that reduces you and your ability to make positive changes, and it can stunt your success.

Our consistent reflections and thought forms can profoundly impact our lives. Negative self-talk can have some astounding impacts. It can fuel anxiety and depression and cause an increase in stress levels while lowering levels of self-esteem. This can lead to decreased motivation as well as greater feelings of helplessness. Decide and take the necessary actions to be bold for positive lasting change in your inner well-being. Remind yourself that thoughts are not facts, set your thoughts into perspective, refrain from a limited thinking pattern – tell yourself you can do it, believe it, and do it. Understand that perfectionism does not exist – glean from setbacks and use the lessons learned for lasting enhanced change rather than hemming yourself in with negative labels. Replace the negative labels with positive affirmations. Replace *"I am a failure"* with *"I am a work in progress," "I can never get it right,"* with *"I will try and fail rather than fail to try,"* and *"It runs in the blood"* with *"I am a different person and not limited to my family history or past."* Negative self-talk can lead to a lowered ability to see opportunities, and a decreased tendency to capitalize on these opportunities.

One of the most apparent disadvantages of negative self-talk is that it's not positive. Research indicates that positive self-talk is a great predictor of success. For example, one study on athletes compared four types of self-talk *(instructional, motivational, positive, and negative)* and found that positive self-talk was the greatest predictor of success. One of my favourite artists is Guy Sebastian. He married a woman he knew while he was growing up. When he became a megastar, I presume the dynamics changed between them, and their marriage experienced a breakup. They reunited and restored what was tarnished. Guy wrote a song for his wife, and it's entitled *"Believer."* I gleaned from the lyrics that his wife dabbled in the arena of negative self-talk. Then the next verse of this song is Guy's comeback with positive affirmations this song has a profound impact on the tugs of the soul and the heartstrings. Here is the song introduction, verse, and pre-chorus:

"Take a deep breath 'cause you're getting ahead of yourself
What gave you the idea, I'd be better off with someone else?
You keep pickin' yourself apart, say you're not good enough
Made up the truth in your mind but if you really mean
The words you just said to me

Then show me a light that shines brighter than your green eyes
And find me a pain that cuts deeper than losin' you

If you think I should leave, sell it to me like a preacher
(Like a preacher, like a preacher)

But you'll never make me, never make me a believer
You are the reason that I believe in myself
The fighter of all of my demons
You love me through Heaven and Hell
From the center to the surface
Every inch is perfect
If you only looked at yourself
Through my eyes, you would see
There's no way that I could leave"

Flagellating yourself for lack of discernment is futile, recognise the lasting impact that negative self-talk is having in your life. Focus on negotiating your mind and not on conflicts per se. Virtues may flounder but resolve to flourish when enlightenment knocks on the door. Pick up the pieces to rebuild. Psychologists regularly assist people in understanding their thoughts and educate and empower them to continue living their lives with a more positive inner dialogue to help them achieve their goals. If you would like to talk more with a psychologist to see what you can learn, reach out to a practitioner you trust. Alternatively, start a conversation with someone you trust.

There are many ways to reduce self-talk in your daily life. Catch your critic before it derails you. Foster self-awareness and learn to notice when you are being self-critical to make a remedial stop. Remember that thoughts and feelings are most certainly not always reality. Contain your negative patterns and build a mechanism to harness your positive emotional resonance. It takes a vast amount of vitality, power, spirit, and energy to manage a perception of the ideal life - give yourself latitude and transcend negativity to neutrality. It's often far easier to change the intensity of your language. *"I can't stand this"* becomes, *"This is challenging." "I hate "* becomes *"I don't like "* and even *"I don't prefer."* Much of your self-talk's negative power is muted when it uses more gentle language. Replace the bad with something good. Align your brain into a rhythmic vigour. We cannot always choose the music life plays for us all, but we can decide how to dance or self-talk to it.

Negative Self Talk

I will always fail

Nothing I do is good enough

I am not smart enough

I only have bad luck

People will never help me

Positive Self Talk

I will succeed

Everything I do is high quality

My knowledge is sufficient

Good things will always happen

My friends are there for me

Creating Your Legacy

"Try and leave this world a little better than you found it, and when your turn comes to die, you can die happy in feeling that, at any rate, you have not wasted your time but have done your best." – Robert Baden-Powell

How do you identify and contain your negative patterns of self-talk?

_____
_____
_____
_____

In what ways do you permit others to influence your worth?

_____
_____
_____
_____

Can you track your success and habits of self-talk?

_____
_____
_____
_____

What are some of the lasting impacts of your negative self-talk, and how will you remedy this?

_____
_____
_____
_____

How do you monitor your stress level and negative self-talk?

_____
_____
_____
_____

Personal Development Goals

Getting Unstuck

Unstuck, the synonyms are released, freed and taken off. The acronym is stuck, wedged, trapped, and imprisoned. At some point in life, we have all felt jammed and obstructed in some shape, way, or form. Identifying the root cause of your frame of mind can help you narrow down your strategies to regain your sense of purpose and forward momentum.

Some common reasons why you might be feeling emotionally and mentally stuck right now are: death, cognitive overload, being overwhelmed, burnout, instability on a personal and global platform, unappreciated and low morale due to poor friendships, and the list goes on. Follow your heart and nurture your mind. Refuse to remain stagnant, especially when life is brusque and restless. Take action, albeit somewhat belatedly – move even at a snail's pace. Revel and believe in the beautiful while straining the contours of your life like a hot knife cutting through butter. The truth is painful, but deciding to own the truth will set you free. Silence and inaction are compliance. Find a tenuous balance between what you can control and cannot. Then sprinkle your magic in every facet of life that you can enhance.

Difficult times can make you feel like you have lost your sense of direction. Weariness can make you feel stuck and uncertain about where to turn from not getting enough rest to living during an unprecedented pandemic. Self-limitation and self-sabotage are often the results of looking for a way out. Whether it's a career, marriage, or friendship you are unfortunate with, you may unconsciously engage in self-sabotaging behaviour. You may also live with impostor syndrome, where you doubt your self-worth and capabilities.

When you live with mental health conditions like depression or anxiety, they may add to your feeling of being stuck. However, when you manage these conditions, yes, indeed, they **can** be managed, and you can regain your motivation and sense of purpose. Transcend shame and stigma, and seek the support you need and deserve. Your choices shape your life from sunrise to sleep, and you control the switch to get stuck or unstuck.

The key lesson here is to stay curious even when that curve ball comes hurling your way. Give yourself the liberty to change the spiel-like costumes. Look forward to what the wind may blow your way and get excited about the change; it's disguised in growth, potential, and strength. Grab it and showcase your potential rather than getting derailed. Turn the negative into a positive. What's your zeal? This is why you must follow through when facing obstacles – find your passion. Understand when your *'keen'* button needs to go on in full blast. Know your values and forge your path – align to your soul's magnetic north. When you follow someone else's path, you will be unfulfilled, and it will lead you to get stuck. You must invest in yourself to pick up your paddles and chart your supreme path. Focus on your day-by-day. Gain perspective; this will support you to select your path and identify your broader vision. A lack of clear goals for your personal and professional life may make you feel stuck.

When you are feeling isolated, or your finances have taken a plummet, this could lead you to feel stuck in life. It is helpful to turn to others for support and reassurance during challenging times. Build a network proactively to have a robust support system when needed. Too often, people do not pay attention to this critical pillar that props life. During the pandemic lockdown, New South Wales, Australia, was shut substantially. My favourite shopping boutique in Lane Cove was shut in compliance with the regulations. One of the employees at this store later mentioned to me how difficult she found it to cope when in lockdown. She had no phone or virtual conversations. No network of friends or support system. She professed that her mental health was not in great shape. Sadly, many others in Australia and other countries suffered the same fate. They had no support network. Let's glean some lessons: be proactive about creating a support network. Be there for others so they can return the favour when you need it. In addition, develop the art of becoming comfortable with your own company. Find things to do and keep yourself engaged and busy. Under normal circumstances, I am a social butterfly and globe-trotting around the world – living to the fullest. Naturally during lockdown, my friends thought I would not cope well with the confinement. On the contrary, I made the most of the cards that were dealt to me. I found my focus on doing things that I normally did not have the time to do. I wrote a bestselling book, read more, cooked more, ate more home-cooked meals, and spent more time with myself. I purged the noise from my life and established better boundaries. I could objectively discern who and what was for me and identify the takers who were sucking the life out of me.

Very early one Saturday morning, I was driving to the dentist, and a message on my car dashboard forever changed my life. It unravelled me in so many profound ways. Stuck is an understatement! Bamboozled, perplexed, and bewildered, I had to find my feet and breath. I also launched my book and rode the crest of that wave, high and joyful. Society informs us that the reality is: you cannot enjoy the ecstasies of life when you are stuck with profound pain. I had to find my equilibrium to get unstuck. It's not an easy path but mandatory for my emotional well-being. To get unstuck, you may want to leave perfectionism, expectations of others, and resentment behind. It's natural to feel conflicted between what you want your life to be and what is dished out to you. Hesitating between one and the other may impede your personal growth and lead to feeling empty. Like a coin has two sides, I needed to accept that life will always have two sides – the good and the bad will visit simultaneously. It is your craft how you manage this.

Sometimes other people get us stuck consciously or unconsciously. We cannot live authentically when others are defining our parameters for life.

The first rule of getting unstuck from lived experience is to 'Define your own life – don't allow others to dictate what is acceptable in your world.' Live for yourself and not for others. Carl Jung once said, *"What you resist persists."* Simply refusing to embrace transformation may keep the sensation of being mentally stuck. Often, we dig in our heels and reject to accept change, injury, transition, loss, or damage and calculated pain that was purposely dispensed. When you devote your energy to fighting the new, you may have difficulty moving forward – don't get stuck. **The wounds are probably not your mistake. However, the decision to heal is your responsibility.**

If you're feeling stuck, it can help first to identify your reasons and then figure out what works to help you remove your barriers. Some techniques to consider:

- ♦ Self-awareness – examine how you unconsciously may be contributing to feeling stuck

- ♦ Identifying your defence mechanisms and cognitive distortions that are getting in your way

- ♦ Notice your default relationship patterns that cause you to recreate familiar cycles

- ♦ Consider finding a therapist to support you and help you tackle challenges

- ♦ Take responsibility – it's natural to fall into the blame game from time to time

- ♦ You can take an honest inventory and find ways to practice forgiveness

- ♦ Cultivate presence – honour the power of NOW

- ♦ You can switch off autopilot by practicing mindfulness techniques to help reroute

- ♦ It may also help to take a step back and make decisions from a place of calm and clarity, rather than amid busyness and chaos

- ♦ Detach from unrealistic expectations – if you tend toward perfectionism, imposter syndrome, or fear of failure, you may want to think of how this is getting in your way.

- ♦ Choose self-love – you can invest in yourself by love. You may want to start by silencing your inner saboteur. Try choosing to be your own best friend rather than your worst critic

- ♦ Create a vision – there are many ways to develop a vision for what you want in life. You can try writing out your strategy. Define professional goals and set an action plan with measurable steps

♦ Living with intention and visualizing what success means to you may help you positively leverage the power of self-fulfilment

♦ Request support – your support network is an important aspect of your well-being. Maybe you can revisit old friendships or establish new ones

♦ Practice healthy detachment – it may be time to reassess your feelings about your current relationship, job, or yourself. What are the aspects that make you feel stuck? Is change possible?

♦ Cultivate inner strength – consider cultivating a mindset that views setbacks, mistakes, and feeling stuck as important parts of learning. Turning these setbacks into opportunities may help you bounce back and then work on more strategies that help you feel unstuck

♦ Find or remember your purpose – working or living without a purpose is often the reason behind feeling stuck. When you get stuck, it's good to re-orient yourself to your goal.

♦ Focus on the journey – while finding your purpose is important, it's equally important to stay in the present and not focus too much on the future

♦ Let go of the past – ask yourself why you are stuck on these memories, and what you can do to live with them, accept them, and move forward

♦ Change your perspective – once you release the grip of the past, you will see your reality in new ways and feel freer to change your attitude.

♦ Start with small changes – change stimulates different parts of the brain that improve creativity and clarity of mind. You can start small by changing your daily routines, moving things around your house, or making new friends. Every choice matters

♦ Believe in yourself – trust that you can reach your expectations and get out of your comfort zone. List your strengths and positive traits, and remember you are competent.

♦ Believing in yourself is to recognize your self-doubt. Pay attention to the ways you react to situations. Then you can work to reframe your self-doubt. Limitations like *"I can't"* or *"I don't know"* can be replaced with *"I can't do that yet, but I'm working on it"* or *"I don't know now, but I will."* Another way to instil confidence in your abilities is to write down your past successes and keep the notes on hand when you need proof that you can do challenging or new things.

- ♦ Practice being hopeful – perhaps you had a lot of disappointments that led to this moment in your life when you feel helpless. Maybe you are experiencing a naturally protective feeling of pessimism. This is something you will have to work to change. Find a practice, such as meditation, prayer, or reading inspirational books, and do it regularly. Hope is not a permanent state. You need to work at it every day.

- ♦ Reassess, improve, and realign many times until you find your blue sky

Getting stuck is common and can happen in any area of your life. The good news is that getting unstuck is entirely possible. Depending on why you are stuck, it can be as easy as finding a new hobby or doing something you have always wanted to try or as difficult as rearranging your entire life and reconsidering your purpose. Either way, getting stuck doesn't mean you're stuck forever. For example, a recent article found that people often get stuck in unsatisfying relationships for reasons like cohabitation, marriage, children, and family entanglement. Similarly, a 2016 article implies that people might be stuck at an unsatisfying or emotionally draining job because of job insecurity. While feeling stuck is generally perceived as something bad, the feelings that come with it can catalyse change. This can ultimately result in something positive.

Recovery can make us feel stuck – stuck in isolation, stuck in guilt – whether legitimate or false, stuck in desolation. The Samaritan woman from The Bible knew something about being stuck. She was stuck in a devastating cycle of loving and losing men. In this grubby rut, Jesus pursues her and pursues us, freeing us to do what we were made to do – to enjoy and glorify God. The lonely Samaritan woman went daily at high noon to draw water, seeking to fill her thirst. She expected to be alone then, to escape the harsh glares of her disapproving community. Imagine her astonishment when a Jewish man crossed the cultural and racial divide to speak to her, a woman, a Samaritan. **She was unstuck**. The Samaritan woman's radical transformation highlights Jesus' mercy when we are stuck in the ruts of recovery – John 4:4–30.

It takes effort to get unstuck
Photograph:
Melbourne, Australia
2022

Creating Your Legacy

"To leave the world a bit better, whether by a healthy child, a garden patch, or a redeemed social condition; To know even one life has breathed easier because you have lived. This is to have succeeded." – Ralph Waldo Emerson

How do you remain alert and ahead of the curve?

_____

_____

_____

_____

In what way do you practice hopefulness?

_____

_____

_____

_____

Do you allow others to define the parameters of your life, and how do you feel about this?

_____

_____

_____

_____

What do you do when you are stuck in a rut?

_____

_____

_____

_____

_____

_____

_____

_____

_____

_____

Personal Development Goals

_____
_____
_____
_____
_____
_____
_____
_____
_____
_____
_____
_____
_____
_____
_____
_____
_____
_____
_____
_____
_____
_____
_____
_____
_____
_____
_____
_____
_____
_____
_____
_____
_____

Forgiveness and Self Respect

It is frequently reasoned that the annoyed and resentment-holding person tends to harm herself, like a scorpion stinging itself to death with its own tail. We are bombarded to forgive. Most of us have stepped up to recognise the merits of forgiveness. Where does your self-respect guide land into the equation to question the atrocity against us? We have erected shrines for war heroes – conduct special tributes to those that fought and survived. Do we not have a right to be angry at those that started the war... where is the recognition for all the other painful facets in the equation? Are they not legitimate emotions? Is it illogical to regard authentic reactions as self-poisoning?

Each of us will occasionally offend those that mean the most to us, we will be presented with periods when we will want to be forgiven by those we have wronged. Granted this, no coherent person would yearn to live in a world where forgiveness was not regarded as a remedial virtue. There are many things to be said in favour of forgiveness: it allows us to show our genuine pledge to love and compassion in difficult situations. Forgiveness does not require recognition; however, humans deserve to be seen and heard. They have a regard for their self-respect when they are mistreated. It is a complex dance to get the balancing act just right. Forgive and heal or let self-respect reign and dictate the path? Forgiving is a chore, and does forgiving at the onset indicate diminished self-respect? Do we need to validate our emotions of pain?

Self-respect may often be shown through begrudging those who spitefully inflict wounds upon us. We display our moral respect for others by feeling annoyance when others are wronged. Have we pondered to express moral respect for ourselves by feeling resentment when we are wronged? And when we do not, what does this show? That we are revealing the intrinsic worth of fondness and forgiveness, or purely that we are submissive beings with little self-esteem, incapable of mandating the respect that we deserve? One of the most intimidating things is our self-respect when we are aggrieved. It is the symbolic message that the culprit seems to be conveying about us – the stigma message that we matter less than the wrongdoer. This is a message that one's self-respect prompts one to resist, and resentment of the wrongdoer is our primary emotional way of expressing such resistance.

The Lady Macbeth syndrome looms large in the moral literature on forgiveness The Lady Macbeth Effect describes a psychological condition in which people who have done something wrong need to wash their hands or body to clear their conscience. They tend to think that physical cleanliness can be a substitute for moral purity. In this era, how often do we see people taking ownership of their conduct? Do they purposefully ponder their actions? Even if they know that they dropped the ball, it's a hard pill for them to swallow and apologize, creating a hornet's nest for unconditional forgiveness. No one has discovered a formula that neglects ambiguity and suppresses doubt.

We try to unravel a symbol of its identity in the facets of everyday life. I have offered love, kindness, dignity, financial help, and business propositions to a woman from international shores I have never met. Handed her a new life on a silver platter. In return, she resorted to gold digging and used my brand to gain commission. Understandably, this left a bad taste in my mouth. Forgiveness left the building; what reigned was a host of emotions from so many evil plots on her part. I had to dig deep to focus on my core values, *"to be a giver,"* and not let the taker's actions or lack of ethics derail me. Life throws us all curve balls. We must work through each layer to find the resolution that brings the fragrance to forgiveness, self-respect, and retribution.

Life is never about holding good cards but rather a decision and action to play the substandard hand with tact and finesse. When you refuse to introspect your behaviour, deeds, and actions, both insignificant and profound, you plummet down south in a period of lethal stalemate – you killed the relationship. An ideology that menaces humanity. Yet we never learn. Don't blame distractions. Instead, improve your focus. Vivacious and vain logic will get you nowhere. If you want to go places, take an inventory of your behaviour, how you tarnish other people's self-respect, and how you bring vengeance to the scene. Refrain from setting the scene for the war and then refusing to eat a humble pie when the sky falls. Swift forgiveness can undermine self-respect, respect for the moral order, respect for the victim, and even respect for forgiveness itself. No one wants *"cheap grace."* Changed behaviour and acknowledgment go the mile instead.

The ethical obligation is not merely a matter of rational assurance; it necessitates demonstrative faithfulness as well, for a moral person is not simply a person who holds the theoretical credence that certain things are incorrect. The moral person is also driven to do something about the wrong. They will also convey emotionally, characteristically, by resentment, that being wronged justly matters and that the wrongdoer should assume a strong adverse response.

Christians support universal and unconditional forgiveness, whereas others maintain that repentance should first be compulsory. These Christians are, not surprisingly, fond of quoting Jesus' remark in Luke 17:3: If thy brother trespasses against thee, rebuke him; and if he repents, forgive him. In John 2:14- 15 where Jesus exhibited virtuous anger and thus imposed disciplinary violence by whipping the money changers in the temple. There is ample constructive significance unearthed in resentment. Then why do these passions suffer such bad press?

Who has not been hurt by the actions or words of another? Perhaps a sibling constantly criticized you growing up, a co-worker damaged a project, or your friend betrayed your trust. Or maybe you have had a traumatic experience, such as being physically or emotionally abused by someone close to you. These lacerations can leave you with ongoing emotions of annoyance and hatred – even retaliation. But if you don't practice forgiveness, you might be the one who pay most profoundly. By implementing forgiveness, you can also embrace peace, optimism, appreciation, and delight. Reflect on how forgiveness can transcend your life and lead you toward physical, emotional, and spiritual well-being.

Have you considered what the effects of holding a grudge are?

+ You may latch onto and take wrath and cynicism into every liaison and new experience

+ You are so steeped in the past and who, what, or how you were wronged that you are unable to enjoy the present

+ You may spiral down into a negative state of depression or nervous breakdown

+ You may dwell on myths that your life is deficient of meaning, purpose, and value

+ You may squander valuable and enriching opportunities and enriching fellowship

Forgiveness is possible – even if reconciliation is not on the horizon. The person you may need to forgive may never change. The eureka moment here is to galvanise that forgiveness is for your benefit. You are the focal point – live your values. The fundamental aspect is to first genuinely evaluate and recognise the offences you brought into the equation. How your behaviour affected others. Introspect – if you are sincerely remorseful, consider admitting it to the one you hurt. Refrain from making excuses for your behaviour. Take ownership, and don't mandate someone to forgive you. Each soul must walk their journey to illumination and become the beacon of light in the vast darkness of unforgiveness.

Unforgiveness keeps you bound like a ball and chain. Forgiveness sets you free!

Creating Your Legacy

"A writer doesn't dream of riches and fame, though those things are nice. A true writer longs to leave behind a piece of themselves, something that withstands the test of time and is passed down for generations." – C.K. Webb

How do you validate your emotions and pain?

_____

_____

_____

_____

What does unconditional forgiveness mean to you?

_____

_____

_____

_____

Do you find it difficult to forgive? Why? Why not?

_____

_____

_____

_____

How did it feel to ask someone to forgive you?

_____

_____

_____

_____

_____

_____

_____

_____

_____

Personal Development Goals

_____
_____
_____
_____
_____
_____
_____
_____
_____
_____
_____
_____
_____
_____
_____
_____
_____
_____
_____
_____
_____
_____
_____
_____
_____
_____
_____
_____
_____
_____
_____
_____
_____
_____

Setting Goals

Goal setting is a practice that begins with sensible consideration of what you want to accomplish and concludes with a great deal of intense work to essentially do it. Sandwiched with some incredibly precise steps that transcend the aspects of attaining every goal. Understanding these actions will allow you to prepare goals that you can embark on. In my book *'Don't Just Fly, SOAR,'* I walk the reader through a comprehensive pathway to goal setting, a core component of vision planning. Reference this book to create, implement, and realise your visions of calculated goal setting.

When you establish goals, they must encourage you; this denotes ensuring that they are valuable to you and that there is benefit in achieving them. When you have little concern about the result, or they are irrelevant in the grand scheme of things, the chances of you adding in the elbow grease to make them happen are unlikely. Motivation is key to achieving goals. Define goals that connect to the high priorities in your life. Without this type of emphasis, you can end up with far too many goals, leaving you too little time to devote to each one. Goal achievement requires dedication; hence to maximize the probability of success, you need to feel a sense of determination and have an *"I can do this"* approach. When you lack this, you risk putting off what you must do to make the goal a reality. This leaves you with a sense of dissatisfaction and exasperation with yourself, both of which are de-motivating. You can end up in a very vicious downward spiral. You need to spend considerable time, energy, and focus to regain your mojo back. You must bolt from the blue to awaken your torpor; the whammy may leave lasting chills in your frame of mind.

Certain people may have difficulty accomplishing their goals because they mix their goals with daily self-improvement efforts. Just because you decide to start watching less television every day – does not necessarily equate to a conscious goal. Goal setting is a purposeful, targeted, and explicit process that starts with identifying a new objective, skill, or project you want to achieve. Then, you make a plan for achieving it, and you work to accomplish it. When you define goals, you can somewhat steer your life's direction. Goals provide you with focus. It presents a rebuttal to unforeseen circumstances when you consider all the risks and mitigation plans. Life may not pan out exactly like your plan; however, you have better resilience to bounce back when you have a snapshot of your goals. You have discernment of what's ahead.

Christmas 2021, my husband and I sojourned to Fiji for the holidays. The entire world was buckling under the strain of prolonged pandemic lockdowns. We planned to spend the festive season in South Africa with my family, and the international border was slammed shut due to the Omicron virus. We scrambled to obtain tickets at the eleventh hour to Fiji. Eventually, we got the mandatory COVID-19 PCR testing and took to the sky. We had a wonderful break and were grateful to travel after such a long lockdown confinement. Before our return trip, we were mandated to repeat the PCR testing to obtain the all-clear tick before our departure. My husband tested positive for COVID-19. Nothing can motivate any person to re-evaluate their strategy and goals like a deadly virus that threatens to end your life.

We were quarantined in the resort. Locked up in a resort on a tropical island. Fiji was hit by a cyclone, and Denarau Island was cut off from the mainland. Electricity and telecommunications were affected. Then, when we thought nothing else could go wrong, Tonga had an emergency. A volcanic eruption in Tonga triggered a tsunami alert for Fiji. We had to brace to prepare for an evacuation in torrential rain while COVID-19 positive. Despite all the catastrophes – none of which we ever envisioned or planned for. We both focused purposefully on what we could control. We targeted and managed our micro daily goals. We accepted what we could not change. We created a routine to give us positive outcomes. We had a cleaning regime to wash all the beddings and clothes daily, wipe down all the surfaces with disinfectant, do steaming with essential oils, use the pulse oximeter to measure blood oxygen levels, and planned activities to pass the day. After a few days, I tested positive, and our 14 days quarantine process had to start from day one yet again. By the end of it, the pair of us were having fun. We defined clear goals; we understood our objectives to *"come out of this alive,"* and so we did. A summary of goals in action – no extravagance but the sheer drive to achieve our desired outcome.

Misguided expectations will never effectively bring any goal in line with reality. Analogous to anticipations, the Real McCoy is perseverance. To ensure your goal is motivating, understand why it's valuable and significant. Accomplishing goals entails profuse emotional bandwidth. Success lives where the mind dwells – align your mind to focus on your core values and objectives. For goals to be prominent, they should be designed to be SMART. There are many variations of what SMART stands for, but the essence is this – goals should be:

- ◆ **S**pecific
- ◆ **M**easurable
- ◆ **A**ttainable
- ◆ **R**elevant
- ◆ **T**ime Bound

Your goal must be well-defined and clear. Ambiguous or generalized goals are unconstructive as they lack adequate focus. Your goals need to highlight the path for you. Create a vision of precisely where you ultimately want to be, then underpin small tasks to help you get closer to your goal each day. Define an action plan and stick to it no matter what unleashes itself. While we were ticking off our goals during the quarantine – we did not squander focus when we received the notification of a tsunami evacuation. Even when you cannot see the forest for the trees – keep going with your planned goals in a structured manner. Eventually, the light will appear at the end of the tunnel. Allow yourself to succeed rather than derailing your future by perceiving the worst outcome.

Short-term objectives are breaking out a long-term goal into more sizable bits:
We created a daily routine to follow in quarantine.

Performance-based goals are short-term objectives set for specific duties or tasks:

We played board games, read, watched movies, and had self-reflection time.

Quantitative goals are evaluated based on numbers or statistics:
We monitored our condition and reduced the steaming and blood oxygen monitoring.

Qualitative goal, this is the type that is felt more than measured:
With the progression of time our health conditions improved, and we felt much better.

Outcome verse process-oriented goals:
Outcome is the result you are aiming for, while process refers to the processes that will lead to the desired outcome if you follow them repeatedly. Process goals are more immediate and tangible, keeping you moving toward your outcome goals.

Warm weather conveys attention of spring voyeurs and leaping bullfrogs. But what happens to frogs in the winter? Do they plan purposefully for every season in their brief life? Absolutely, hence what deters us then when we are the more accomplished species? Fortunately for the amphibians, they don't freeze to death. Temperatures must dip slightly below 32 degrees Fahrenheit to freeze a frog, and ice begins to grow when an ice crystal touches the frog's skin.

Regardless, these amphibians don't just turn into a slab of ice. A sequence of processes ensues to safeguard the death of the frog. Minutes after ice forms in the skin, the frog's liver begins converting sugars, stored as glycogen, into glucose. This sugar is released from the liver and carried through the bloodstream to every tissue, where it helps keep cells from completely dehydrating and shrinking. As the frog is freezing, its heart continues pumping the protective glucose around its body. The frog's heart slows and eventually stops. All other organs stop functioning. The frog stops breathing and appears to be dead. When the weather gets warmer, the frog melts. The frog has to go through a repair process. Even the frog has clearly defined soul goals to keep it alive. Nature found a way.

Are you finding your way to survive your winter with the goals you must set? Sometimes we also need to stop functionalities that keep our core goal of survival alive. Leap forward and set your goals that will warrant your thriving.

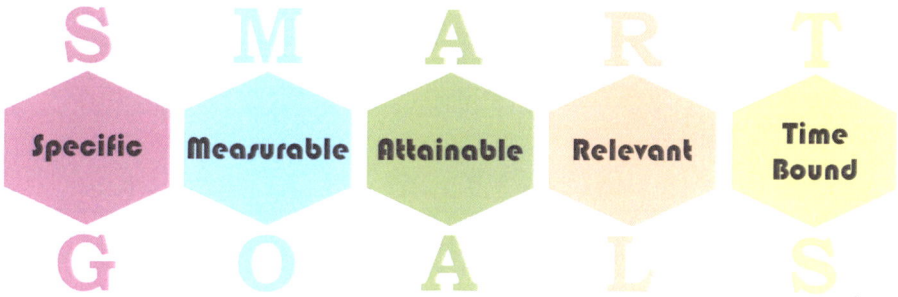

S   M   A   R   T

| Specific | Measurable | Attainable | Relevant | Time Bound |

G   O   A   L   S

Creating Your Legacy

"We all die. The goal isn't to live forever, the goal is to create something that will." – Chuck Palahniuk

What system do you use to set, measure and achieve goals?

_____

_____

_____

_____

How do you keep yourself motivated?

_____

_____

_____

_____

Can you foresee risk and plan for it?

_____

_____

_____

_____

What do you prefer to achieve in life?

_____

_____

_____

_____

_____

_____

_____

_____

_____

_____

_____

Personal Development Goals

_____
_____
_____
_____
_____
_____
_____
_____
_____
_____
_____
_____
_____
_____
_____
_____
_____
_____
_____
_____
_____
_____
_____
_____
_____
_____
_____
_____
_____
_____
_____
_____

Building Habits

A habit is a recurrent, often unconscious pattern of behaviour that is acquired through frequent repetition: like making a habit of getting up early. Constantly purchasing the same perfume brand **out of** (= because of) habit. Sometimes we struggle to **get into** (= start) the habit of not eating too many donuts before dinner. According to a 2009 study published in the European Journal of Social Psychology, a person takes 18 to 254 days to form a new habit. The study also concluded that, on average, it takes 66 days for a new behaviour to become automatic. Some people are better apt to form habits than others. A consistent routine of any kind is not everyone's cup of tea.

When asked how long it takes to form a habit, many people will respond, *"21 days."* This notion can be traced back to *"Psycho-Cybernetics,"* a book published in 1960 by Dr. Maxwell Maltz. Dr. Maltz did not make this claim but referenced this number as an observable metric in both himself and his patients. He wrote: *"These, and many other commonly observed phenomena, tend to show that it requires a minimum of about 21 days for an old mental image to dissolve and a new one to gel."* But as the book became more popular — more than 30 million copies have been sold — this situational observation has become accepted as fact. It's a misnomer, so refrain from falling into that trap.

Our habit's structure and shape who we are. Admittedly, forming positive habits is not always comfortable. Depending on whether they are healthy or negative habits. Habits regulate if we are joyful or ill-fated. Healthy or unhealthy. Exhausted or well-rested. Strong or frail. The power of habits is far-reaching. Habits are the nature of our attitudes, actions, and decision-making abilities. And they affect every aspect of our lives. A good habit will help you reach your goals and develop personal and professional strengths. However, not all habits are good. Habits are such a mercurial mix. You must be strategic about what you nurture and purge in this bag of tricks. A reward-seeking mechanism in the brain drives habits. They are often triggered by something specific. For instance, walking past a fast-food outlet and smelling Kentucky Fried Chicken. I was also a devoted vegetarian for five years. That smell made me buckle, and I forgot my values to quit eating meat. I was triggered by that familiar aroma that I resisted oh so well, many times. In essence, this was not really my recent habit of munching on KFC, however, it was a past routine that I enjoyed. The tug on the brain can sometimes be stronger than our willpower.

The main difference between a habit and a routine is awareness. Both are regular, repeated actions. But while habits run on autopilot, routines are intentional. Routines need deliberate practice, or they will eventually die out. But a habit happens with little or no conscious thought. For instance, we need to apply the attitude of being grateful, reading, creating time for our loved ones, and actively learning something new every day – this is not fuelled on autopilot mode. We need to plan this routine deliberately. Our routine can attract both admiration and scorn. Be true to yourself; you set the pace, not those around you. However, an established custom is a habit, its repeated patterns of behaviour that an individual acquires by their own free will: like complaining, nagging, introspection, respecting the time and not showing up late, authenticity and honesty, and the list goes on. Good habits are important because, once established, habits are often repeated such that they can produce significant results over time.

Do you know how Jane Austen, Benjamin Franklin, and Franz Kafka spent their days? It turns out they had some pretty interesting daily habits, which you should intensely consider pirating. Based on the book *Daily Rituals: How Artists Work,* we gain insights into a pretty fascinating infographic of the daily habits of some of history's greatest writers, composers, and other creatives. Not all of these are great advice – many of the intellectuals smoked a pipe frequently, drank way too much coffee, and ate debatable cuisine – however, amply, some of their habits are worth noting and including in your own life.

Refrain from giving in to another maudlin bout and adopt the art of napping. Research has confirmed that *"sleeping on it"* really does work. Napping has a lot of great benefits, especially for creatives. And while catching a few moments of rest midday may be perceived as lazy, it can be way better for productivity than trying to soldier through a particularly sleepy afternoon. Another gem is sharing your work; the desire to keep your ideas and work to yourself is strong among creatives, but as we learned from David Allen, *"Your head is for having ideas, not holding them."* Maya Angelou read her daily work to her husband every night. Consider letting some of your friends or loved ones in on your projects. The art of being social depicts some of history's greatest thinkers regularly visiting and dining with their friends, which can help fend off the sometimes-crippling loneliness. Our social lives are often the first things that get the axe when we are busy – don't let that happen. Cultivate better habits.

Another pillar to establish, even though it may technically be routine, is to get in the trend to read. This is especially important if you are a writer, but even Beethoven took time out every day to read the paper. Find fine inspiration in all genres and forms. Great habits are cultivated. Even when Nelson Mandela was in prison, he took time to exercise and keep his mental, physical, and emotional health balanced and positive. Cultivate that habit no matter how daunting it may seem; the established habit will pay dividends. When life throws you a curveball, having a rebuttal in hand is great. Set goals, find your purpose, create a vision plan, or define the legacy you wish to leave. Having a plan and measuring your achievements or lack of it is a great habit. Positive habits start with a plan to head north.

Even God rested on the seventh day – the Sabbath. It is a wise habit to program yourself to rest at regular intervals. Take time to rejuvenate. Let the brain fog lift. Just chill and hit reset every day at some point in your day. Form a habit of great sleep hygiene by turning off devices and removing them from the bedroom. Unwind before you go to bed. We get the best from habits when we adjust our attitude. We need to be proactive and discover how to cultivate wholesome habits. Transcending your mindset begins with your attitude. Change occurs when you stop wishing and start doing; that's the beginning of a positive habit. Another powerful approach to cultivating positive habits is to own your mistakes. Refrain from consistently making up bad excuses for poor behaviour. It is critical to identify your mistakes to take charge and create positive habits. Comprehend that this is a marathon, not a sprint. Statistically, it takes 66 days for habits to become second nature. Give yourself the opportunity to cultivate better habits. When you fail, try again; creating new habits requires a steadfast commitment.

Habits permit creative capacity. When former U.S. President Barack Obama was asked why he wears the same suit every day, he replied: "I'm trying to pare down my decisions. I don't want to make decisions about what I'm eating or wearing. Because I have too many other decisions to make." Barack Obama adopted a strict regimen for all the "little things" to ensure he could focus on the big things. This is the evolutionary purpose of habit. We are triggered to do and learn how to do many things subconsciously to free up more of our higher brain level brain activity for important things, such as inventing hybrid cars, building rockets, and creating innovative systems. So, if you want to develop habits that help enable success, focus on habits that help you eliminate the small decisions that we make every day. Commit to habits that see decision made in advance. Probably one of the best habits to try and develop for pretty much everyone is around what we eat. Research shows that most people make around 200 food and eating-related decisions daily. That is a lot of decisions and one of the reasons that diets are so hard to stick to. As a result, a strict eating plan can help you feel better and give you more capacity to think. Harnessing the power of habits is a great way to pursue success. Committing to habits frees up your brain's capacity to make better decisions, do your best work when you are in a prime mental state, and stay on track even when things are difficult. You can take a step in either direction.

Creating Your Legacy

"While it is well enough to leave footprints on the sands of time, it is even more important to make sure they point in a commendable direction." – James Cabell

List all your negative habits.

_____

_____

_____

_____

Are you actively aware of your blind spots?

_____

_____

_____

_____

What habits do you prefer to create?

_____

_____

_____

_____

Can you identify the patterns that keep you stuck?

_____

_____

_____

_____

Have you tried to stop a negative habit? What was the result?

_____

_____

_____

_____

_____

Personal Development Goals

_____
_____
_____
_____
_____
_____
_____
_____
_____
_____
_____
_____
_____
_____
_____
_____
_____
_____
_____
_____
_____
_____
_____
_____
_____
_____
_____
_____
_____
_____
_____
_____
_____
_____

Time Versus Energy

With the progression of time, I have heard many South African citizens complain of pathetic circumstances of living with restrictions of load shedding. The constraints left them with limited time to accomplish their daily task; chasing their tail around electricity depleted their energy levels. No pun intended! Strained at the seams, reshuffled at times, and tattered by the roller-coaster of trying to keep up-to-date. No time for any recuperation at all. This situation piqued my attentiveness to dive deeper into the concept and reality of time versus energy.

The South African electricity crisis, most notably manifesting in successive rounds of *load-shedding*, is an ongoing period of widespread national-level rolling blackouts as electricity supply falls behind electricity demand, threatening to destabilize the national power grid. It began in the later months of 2007 and continues to the present. The South African government-owned national power utility and primary power generator, Eskom, and various parliamentarians attributed these rolling blackouts to insufficient generation capacity.

The struggle economically has continued to endure endemic corruption and authoritarianism in South Africa. We all need support and challenge to keep growing but this crisis gave new meaning to every citizen's schedule, time, and personal energy. Furloughing with unprecedented stress. Granted that the cards handed out are a poor hand to play. Synchronised grace can still tame this beast or any situation in life when we manage time and energy effectively. Suspend whatever assignment engrosses you and refocus on where you spend your time and how you squander your energy. Resist the urge to impulse to an instant fix. You will self-depreciate when you live without understanding the correlation between time versus energy. It would be a serious self-abnegation of guidance if you do nothing to introspect and self-regulate.

When you take care of the days, the months will take care of itself. Are you continually short on time and persistently low on energy? You can be the best time manager in the world but never get anything done if you neglect your energy management. You are acutely aware that time is finite (you only have 24 hours per day). The fact is that time is continuous: it simply resets every 24 hours. Time itself does not alter your state of being – it does not fuel or diminish your energy. You cannot control time. What you do control and what matters is what you do with it. Whether you use time proactively or not, time is simply a constant. Energy is something that you can control, and you can contour it to your needs. We all have to-do lists, and the more we take off, the more we associate that with productivity. Harvard Business

Review mentions, *"Time management skills are among the most desired workforce skills but at the same time among the rarest skills to find."*

They say if you want something done, ask a busy person, even though this idea is somewhat paradoxical. How is it that someone with a mile-long to-do list is usually more likely also to be able to knock off any additional tasks thrown at them – whereas someone with just one or two things to get done in a day might not get around to doing any of them? Great achievers and people with chock-full lives have a good sense of exactly how long things take, how much can fit in any given day or week, and how much they currently have on their plates. They have mastered the art of accomplishing tasks within specified time frames.

Energy is also limited; energy is a resource that needs to be renewed every single day. Unlike the continuity of time, energy is a resource that depletes and withers with the day. What you do with your energy does matter. Whether you make use of it or not, your energy will deplete. Why has society zoomed in and become so obsessed with managing time rather than effectively managing energy? Granted that you can control your energy levels but have no control over time. You can optimize your daily schedule and fine-tune it to the most minute detail, but your efficiency will plunge at the end of the day, and you will get nothing done if your energy is subdued. You can add the verve back into the equation regardless of load shedding, restricted time, daylight saving, or whatever the gamut is.

Isaiah 40:28-31 – *"Have you not known? Have you not heard? The Lord is the everlasting God, the Creator of the ends of the earth. He does not faint or grow weary; his understanding is unsearchable. He gives power to the faint, and to him who has no might, he increases strength. Even youths shall faint and be weary, and young men shall fall exhausted; but they who wait for the Lord shall renew their strength; they shall mount up with wings like eagles; they shall run and not be weary; they shall walk and not faint."* The scripture beautifully confirms that we can renew our strength, the energy whenever we feel depleted. The simplest but effective strategy is to pray and ask God to restore your energy.

When you are physically exhausted because sleep eludes you, you will not have the energy to accomplish what you are required to do. Research has proven that poor sleep translates into poor productivity and performance. It's not proper time management that improves your efficiency. It is appropriate energy management that stands the test of time. You have to pay cautious attention to five facets that you need when it comes to managing your daily energy:

Physical: This involves getting 7-8 hours of sleep every night, exercising 3-4 times per week, and eating healthy meals. These factors contribute (or do not) to your productivity in life.

Mental: This involves having a clear, focused, and present mind. Grasp the power of now and live in the moment.

Emotional: Emotional intelligence plays a role. You need to be aware of your emotions. Angst, resentment, misery, or even delight, none of them will be conduits to getting things done. The mood is the simple memo: manage your mood and emotional state to be industrious.

Spiritual: This includes any pursuit that nurtures your soul. It might be praying, being in nature, listening to music, or travelling.

Social: Reserved or outgoing, or someone who lies anywhere in between, socializing can have an astonishing influence on your energy – we are social creatures born for fellowship. The whole world felt the plight of mental mayhem when the lockdown forced humanity to give up our social calendar and live in quarantine.

Refrain from trying to manage time. Optimizing your schedule may win the battle but certainly not the war. Instead, master how to manage your energy. Introspect and confirm what is exhausting you and watch what is revitalizing you. Find what fills your cup:

- Manage your physical energy, and you will have a healthy body.

- Manage your mental energy, and you will have a strong mind.

- Manage your emotional energy, and you will have a positive mood.

- Manage your spiritual energy, and you will have a wholesome soul.

- Manage your social energy, and you will have beneficial relationships.

Managing your energy efficiently is what leads to a healthy life. A healthy life is what facilitates a productive one. Honour the laws of fair exchange within yourself and prioritise taking care of yourself. Analyse what you need to change right now to support yourself better. Routinely ask yourself, what do you need to change in your life to do your finest work? Confirm what you need to do right now to shine at your brightest. Zoom into a regular to-do list to be energised. Schedule that weekend escape, that dream holiday, chill with Netflix, pig out on ice cream, have a coffee date, play golf with friends, or simply curl up by the fire with your favourite book. Committing to your dreams and purpose begins with committing to yourself, and productivity means squat if you are in no shape to show up energised and ready to slay. Remember to take care of yourself because your flow is everything, and your well-being is not just a preference but a foundation for the rest of your life. The ebb and flow of your future will ultimately stand the test of time.

The rituals and behaviours you can establish to manage your energy better may transform your life. Set an earlier bedtime and give up drinking, fix any sleeping disorders, take that walk, exercise, and do something extraordinary for someone. Establishing simple rituals like these can produce striking results with your energy levels. Take intermittent breaks for renewal; this results in higher and more sustainable performance. When people can take more control of their emotions, they can improve the quality of their energy, regardless of the external pressures they face. Confronted with relentless demands and unexpected challenges, people tend to slip into negative emotions. They become short-tempered and provoked or restless and uncertain. Such states of mind drain people's energy and cause friction in their relationships. These emotions also make it impossible to think evidently, rationally, and contemplatively. When you recognize what events trigger your negative emotions, you will gain greater capacity to take control of your reactions and manage your energy level effectively.

People can cultivate positive energy by learning to change the stories they tell themselves about the events in their lives. Learn to narrate the most hopeful stories possible. The most effective way to change a story is to view it through any of three new lenses, all of which are alternatives to seeing the world from the victim's perspective. With the *reverse lens*, for example, people ask themselves, *"What would the other person in this conflict say, and in what ways might that be true?"* With the *long lens,* they ask, *"How will I most likely view this situation in six months?"* With the *wide lens,* they ask themselves, *"Regardless of the outcome of this issue, how can I grow and learn from it?"* Each of these lenses can help people intentionally cultivate more positive emotions.

Time and money will run out, but you can replenish your energy and be wise with pursuing what grips you.

Creating Your Legacy

"We stand our best chance of leaving a legacy to those who want to learn, our children, by standing firm. In matters of style, hey, swing with the stream. But in matters of principle, you need to stand like a rock." – Kevin Costner

Do you manage your resources efficiently?

_____
_____
_____
_____

Do you spend most of your time playing catch up? Why? Why not?

_____
_____
_____
_____

In what ways do you use your organizational skills?

_____
_____
_____
_____

Do you plan ahead?

_____
_____
_____
_____

How do you normally cope in emergencies?

_____
_____
_____
_____
_____

Personal Development Goals

_____
_____
_____
_____
_____
_____
_____
_____
_____
_____
_____
_____
_____
_____
_____
_____
_____
_____
_____
_____
_____
_____
_____
_____
_____
_____
_____
_____
_____
_____
_____
_____
_____

Gratitude and Growth

There is a correlation bridge between both gratitude and growth. Your attitude exemplifies so much in your world. You can glean so much in every context – the good and the bad times. A key component of gratitude is understanding: of self and the world around you. Proactively practicing to live life with a sense of gratitude is how you keep growth churning. *"Change is the only constant."* What are you changing from? Growth is moving from a great place to a better place. Those who refuse to learn from their experiences, disappointments, and valuable feedback will never grow into a healthier version of themselves. When gratitude lives in your heart and pumps growth to your veins, your elocution will instantly grace the room and upgrade the atmosphere. The portrait of gratitude and quickened growth will spell your appreciation for resilience and managing that challenge with finesse. When you are recalcitrant – your character will tell a greater tale.

Have you ever pondered what stimulated growth in you? Whatever had a curious influence over you? How are you escorted to the proverbial table with pompous humility? When do you appear pale, proud, pleased, and indifferent by preference or expression? Are you growing in a lane that is complacent? In my value system, growth and gratitude are matched by words spoken and dispatched by actions taken. We are mostly revered for our deeds. When you offer lip service, society can see the results when the rubber hits the road. Manipulation in any way, shape, or form will stunt growth and diminish gratitude. Your character cheerfully attests to its success. When you seek a desired outcome, ensure your growth and gratitude tank can handle the risk and the rewards that come packaged.

Like most humanity, I watched Joe Biden's inaugural speech with intent, and I must attest that the words were profound. In January 2021, the Capitol made an impression – exhibiting growth, and I was most grateful for that. These lines profoundly affected me: ***"A cry for racial justice some 400 years in the making moves us. The dream of justice for all will be deferred no longer. A cry for survival comes from the planet itself. A cry that can't be any more desperate or any clearer."***

Finally, a breath of fresh air – I perceived that gratitude and growth would envelop the landscape in a profound way. How do a country, nation, and world grow? How do we develop gratitude in the hearts of people? Are our leaders leading by example? Do they model growth and gratitude? Do they give us a reason to celebrate and be grateful while we grow in profound ways ourselves? It was a gracefully thin reed to be suspended from – to live by example. How to get out of your way! Our world does not grow from a mere speech or introduction of legislation. It requires more elbow grease than that to move those permanent mountains. I was eerily reminiscent of President Joe Biden's inauguration speech.

Up where we belong, we knew exactly what his speech meant. My gratitude gauge broke when I heard this news on CNN: *"The Florida Department of Education has announced that the state rejected more than 50 math textbooks from next school year's curriculum, citing references to critical race theory among reasons for the rejections. The news release said the list of rejected books makes up approximately 41% of submissions, which is the most in Florida's history. Reasons for rejecting textbooks included references to critical race theory, 'inclusions of Common Core, and Social Emotional Learning (SEL) in mathematics,' the release states. Florida banned the teaching of critical race theory in schools in June 2021."*

We see the chronic dysfunction currently in literature internationally. I have the greatest contempt for pessimism and the most familiar terms with the rut. Astonishingly, the United States of America President made his inaugural speech in January 2021, and in June 2021, Florida decided to ban race theory in schools. I struggle to see the demonstrated bridge of growth and gratitude. If that was unclear, the sentiment was certainly unmistakable. Organisations, society, friendships, and networks can lose the desire for growth and gratitude when we are constantly dispensed with a bitter gall to drink from. You can lose a loved one, an employee, a contract, or something greater when growth and gratitude are not the fabric of your narrative. Refusing to monitor your gratitude and growth will result in poor engagement and bleak results for your future.

Those that invest in growth and plant the seed of gratitude create a brighter future and profoundly increase productivity and engagement. Lucrativeness and human emotions are most definitely complex equations. However, we create a greater vortex when we make promises and do not deliver. Every trace of growth and gratitude will vanish promptly. Humans want to be treated with dignity and respect. Like plants that thrive under the correct conditions, so too do humans. Don't demand growth and gratitude from a person or humanity when your actions do not foster that behaviour. The ability for anyone to feel engaged and appreciated stems from how they are treated. You reap what you sow. When will our world align to true growth and gratitude, not just eloquent speeches? No more false promises. Are you operating in a silo with a tainted vision and expecting growth and gratitude? Does your chronicle include collaboration and empathy?

Resembling all cultural modifications, the change must begin at the top and filter down through individual levels. To those thirsty for a remedy, bring new trends and habits to the chamber – if you want gratitude and growth to be a part of the culture and ecosystem, you must practice it often and consistently. Neutralizing with gratitude magnifies the *'happy juice'* hormones serotonin and dopamine are doused with no formal prescription. When done organically, it becomes part of the culture that lifts all lives. Ethos is critical in the long, two-way street of growth and gratitude. The essential obligation is respect. Honesty is still the best policy. You and those around you will thrive in a place of gratitude and growth. You will have the ability to resolve any catastrophe.

Even when the government unleashes psychological hazards, you can choose your fabric of gratitude and growth pattern. Step up and shrink the gap. Become part of the solution and watch those *'happy juices'* pour out in a torrent. Literature highlights different factors that facilitate or hinder. Which natural effervescent are you? You don't have to dig deep to find treasure here. Your character leaves every room lingering with your gratitude and growth factor in the same fashion that the President's inauguration speech speaks louder than words. Gratitude is a super emotion that enhances many facets of life. Ensure you have prescribed gratitude so you can harness these benefits.

Why GRATITUDE is a SUPER EMOTION

- Reduces Depression
- Strengthens Resiliency
- Less Chronic Pain
- Increased Self-Esteem
- More Likely to Help Others
- Improves Sleep
- Retain More Positive Experiences
- Increases Energy Levels
- Reduces Feelings of Jealousy
- Improves Physical Health

Creating Your Legacy

"I think the whole world is dying to hear someone say, 'I love you.' I think that if I can leave the legacy of love and passion in the world, then I think I've done my job in a world that's getting colder and colder by the day." – Lionel Richie

Do you take the opportunity to appreciate what you have?

_____
_____
_____
_____

In what way are you stunted in life?

_____
_____
_____
_____

List the areas of your life that you require more development in.

_____
_____
_____
_____

How do you express gratitude?

_____
_____
_____
_____
_____
_____
_____
_____
_____
_____

Personal Development Goals

_____
_____
_____
_____
_____
_____
_____
_____
_____
_____
_____
_____
_____
_____
_____
_____
_____
_____
_____
_____
_____
_____
_____
_____
_____
_____
_____
_____
_____
_____
_____
_____

Self-Love and Self-Reflection

I recently came around a table where someone lied to me several times, abused me, and caused me incomprehensible trauma. Yet the discussion was centred around how this narcist is a victim of my reactions. The others around the table demanded that I ignore all the indiscretions and still show respect because that is what the word of God says. It certainly was a round table with buffoons. No command of the word of God or self-love and self-respect.

Self-love is a state of appreciation for oneself that grows from actions that support our physical, psychological, and spiritual growth. Self-love means having a high regard for your well-being and happiness. Self-love means caring for your needs and not sacrificing your well-being to please others. Self-respect is proper respect for oneself as a human being and regard for one's standing or position.

Self-respect can be challenging to practice if you are a people-pleaser. The fear of saying no can keep you stuck in a cycle of abandoning your needs and giving in to things that do not serve you. When we allow others to take advantage of us, we chip away at our self-esteem, which leads to more angst, less interpersonal efficiency and depreciates our self respect. Even those who practice interpersonal effectiveness find themselves in situations that prompt them to relinquish their self-respect. Never let anyone corrode your boundaries, no matter how hurt you are or how hard it is. Dismantling your self-love and self-respect will decompose your journey to contentment.

At this round table discussion, I noticed I was about to let people take advantage of me. But I asserted myself to bring my self-worth to the table. I was hurt immensely, but I walked stronger than before. Each time you stand up for what's just, you respect yourself.

When others take advantage of you, it can generate anger which may lead to:

- Uncompromising reactions and aggressive outbursts.

- Emotions of incompetence and fortifying the false belief that you do not merit respect.

- Aptly ignite you to feel a consciousness of self-awareness and aid you to act boldly. This will help you cultivate robust self-esteem and more self-respect; it takes ample practice and leads to appealing outcomes.

Standing up for yourself can feel uncomfortable, but it pays dividends. When you begin this cycle and develop boundaries, you learn to value yourself and your self-worth. Boundaries are beyond important in the development of self-respect. Some people are an institution in themselves for demanding how others treat them but not considering what they bring to the equation. How does it feel to be mistreated? How did this make you feel? Reflect and understand your emotions. Do not negotiate your worth without anyone. Your value dwells in your heart. Live it. You can get away with adding straws for so long, and then you cannot. Get defiant about insults to your soul.

A requiem to the bygone helps to move forward to a new season – everyone appreciates a fresh meal rather than leftovers. Think coherently and create organic connections that enhance your self-worth. Pay attention to the details – does your network act with integrity? Do they display more pride with doses of ego rather than seeking to keep their self-respect tacked?

In order to develop self-respect, you have to act on it. You show others how you want to be treated by your actions and words. Show them that you are valuable by speaking up and setting strong boundaries. When you have a captivated audience, there is no introduction required. The same analogy is applicable when you have a grounded foundation with self-respect, contentment flows on. Refrain from allowing any trivia to deter you from what brings you ultimate joy. Occasionally self-love is not about admiring yourself. Sometimes self-love is also not about being your cheerleader. Understand the distinctions. Don't trade your authenticity for approval. Self-love means that we should jeer deeper. Invigorating your own heart, unwrapping the layers. It's about having the audacity to look at the bits of yourself that you don't like and unpacking the reason as to why. Sometimes self-love is having the courage to be honest with yourself and paying attention to your mistakes, the areas you need to grow, and how you hope to change. Sometimes self-love means having the courage to admit your failures and then forgive yourself for making them, too. You should love yourself. You should lift yourself. You should cultivate a relationship rooted in admiration, affirmation, and love within your body, mind, heart, and soul.

A day can feel like a lifetime when the heart breaks into many pieces. Use your tools and your wisdom to shield your self-respect. Assess what's not working in your life, physical health, work, relationships, mental health, and the whole gamut. Self-reflection is a necessary component of progress. When you are disgruntled in your relationships, or they do not confidently fuel your sense of worth. This is most definitely a red flag for your self-love and self-respect. Authentic connection requires elbow grease. Others will not love or respect you if you do not love and respect yourself first. Sometimes the world is too busy to notice your voids. You need to champion your path. Seek the balm to your soul. I read, take reflective walks, listen to music, and articulate myself with my expressive pen – writing and a massage. Realign your inner compass.

Fragmented pieces of life are difficult to navigate however, so much equity originates and spurs self-respect. From the ashes, beauty is crafted. In those tears, you learn to sink, swim, or drown. Those intense sentiments create your personal brut, your heartbreak teaches you new ways to love, and rejections harness you to accept others. You can trace nuances in a heartbeat. This story tells your self-love is like the rock of Gibraltar. Empathy is your companion; you understand the circumstances even from unspoken words. You know how to dish out self-respect to yourself and others. Contentment is a reflection of your self-worth, self-love, and self-re spect.

You are
so much
More...

...than the reflection in the mirror.

Creating Your Legacy

"Legacy is not leaving something for people. It's leaving something in people." – Peter Strople

How do you love yourself?

_____
_____
_____
_____

How often do you introspect your life, choices, and contentment levels?

_____
_____
_____
_____

When did you stand up for yourself?

_____
_____
_____
_____

Define what self-respect is to you?

_____
_____
_____
_____
_____
_____
_____
_____
_____
_____
_____

Personal Development Goals

_____
_____
_____
_____
_____
_____
_____
_____
_____
_____
_____
_____
_____
_____
_____
_____
_____
_____
_____
_____
_____
_____
_____
_____
_____
_____
_____
_____

Women of Distinction

As a young lass, I recall my dad purchasing a shining pair of blue shoes with gorgeous bows on it for me. I loved it and felt the wonderment of a little princess when I slipped them on, but that fairy tale toppled when my brother pushed me, then stomped on my new shoes and feet. He yelled, *"And now you have another pair of shoes."* I seriously did not have a vast collection at that stage; however, his brutal reaction shocked me into a realization that we were infinitely different. I was female and gleaned the fact that I will always have more shoes than he ever will. Women are cut from a different cloth. If the chaos of life can be organized and put into a bento box, there strides a woman in her natural element. She is vulnerable to create from any void. The essential essence of a woman is kindness in a mother, a fervent wife, a considerate daughter, a trustworthy sister, a balanced professional, and a dependable friend. A woman personifies ageless beauty, selfless love, and profound dignity.

As a woman of colour, the gap for others to stereotype is set and presented at many international tables I sat at. It is a mammoth effort to revive an eighteenth-century mindset with a twenty-first-century vision. I had to dig deep to seek solace in myself and not demand a prescriptive approach but be solutions-oriented. To proactively blend into my landscape, then conquer the parameters set to hem me in – the unflinching eyes of a zealot, a woman's intuition. Around the globe, we celebrate and recognize achievements made by prominent women – a great practice. Another glow-up is distinguishing your journey. Where you started, how you impact the world, what difference you make to others, and the direction you are heading towards. It is vital to empower yourself, as it is essential to the health and social development of families, communities, and countries. When women live safe, fulfilled, and productive lives, they can reach their full potential. Contributing their skills to the workforce makes a profound difference to society and can raise happier and healthier children – our future leaders.

Let's deal with the facts and not opinions: from a global perspective, educational inequality is one of women's biggest challenges. Despite the many gains of modern feminist movements in America, Africa, Asia, and beyond, many still believe that women are less worthy of the same educational opportunities afforded to men. **Ladies, it's up to us to make a material difference and impact the world profoundly and subtly.**

"Dreams don't turn to gold, and there's just no easy way," echoed so beautifully in Whitney Houston's song. As a battle-tested leader, I know from experience when life looks like a train wreck, that's just the beginning. It is not the main act to confess defeat and get derailed. Kamala Harris is a

Democratic U.S. senator from California, and she has made it to the table to be seen and heard. However, not all cultures and countries offer women the same opportunities. Some families starve their female children and give all the opportunities to the male children. Women are disadvantaged from the womb. Lasses, we got this; shake off the limitation's others have carved out for us. Establish your boundaries and goals. The extremely potent combination of sexism, racism, and economic inequality – even if this may seem too broad to overcome in your current landscape. Find your equilibrium and set the pace. Even when the narrative is against you, we can change the outcomes. One choice and day at a time. Do not allow the train wreck to define you, be the force of salvage. In many ways, we are not just doing as well as men. We are surpassing them.

One of the most prominent women in our era is Oprah Winfrey. Her life did not begin in the limelight with golden handshakes. She is the classic example of changing the chronicle we are born into. The onus is up to you and me and not the big personalities. Seventy percent of the 1.3 billion people living in conditions of poverty are women. In urban areas, 40 percent of the poorest households are headed by women. In addition, women predominate in the world's food production by 50-80 percent, but they own less than 10 percent of the land. Let us focus on the opportunities, solutions, and closing the gaping gaps. Even more disconcerting, in too many places around the globe, women exercising or even seeking their basic rights is interpreted as a direct and destabilizing challenge to existing power structures. We all need to join the voices of women leaders worldwide, challenging governments, the private sector, and civil society to revive and reinvest in the policies and in the legal and social frameworks that will achieve worldwide gender equality and inclusion. Use your voice to STOP the wreck. Whether these forces succeed will depend on you and everyone standing to be seen and heard. Recognizing the urgency and peril of inaction is critical.

A fundamental shift is encouraging the use of gender-inclusive language means speaking and writing in a way that does not discriminate against a particular sex and does not perpetuate gender stereotypes. Given the key role of language in shaping cultural and social attitudes, using gender-inclusive language is a powerful way to promote gender equality and eradicate gender bias. Allow yourself to work in concert to get this ball rolling, especially in male-dominated faculties. Another fostering behavioural shift is respecting the woman in a professional work setting. I work in medical Information Technology – a predominantly male division sector, two decades ago. Men would swear and act like they were in a barn. Mothers let us groom our men to respect women and professional boundaries. **Don't let the train wreck define you; develop the art to paint your scene regardless of the circumstances.**

How do I empower myself as a woman? There are a series of guidelines that you can carry out to work on your empowerment and become a vested woman:

♦ Distinguish yourself and respect who you are. Frame your character narrative.

♦ Enhance your persona. Establish goals and actively work on them.

♦ Get out of your comfort zone, and challenge yourself each day.

♦ Bring out the best in others, and cultivate valuable relationships.

♦ Build a network of contacts, and find support and camaraderie.

♦ Be yourself, show up authentically, and foster a real sisterhood.

♦ Work on your self-confidence, groom, glean, grow, and glow in every season of life.

♦ Educate yourself; knowledge conquers ignorance.

Being a woman means having a robust sense of identity, being tolerant of your body as one that adapts and changes over time, being confident, and building up the people in your life. It means you have the wisdom to be grateful for what you have while still hungry enough for growth. It's growth when you dress up how you want to be addressed – insight. An authentic woman feeds herself, covers all the needs in the household, and doesn't go around asking other people. A most respected woman does not need anything from other people. She just depends on herself. She is the one who struggles for everything that she needs. **Becoming a Proverbs 31 woman** is not as hard as you think. Proverbs 31 *is* not a checklist or a to-do list. Instead, it's a beautiful representation of what it means to be a virtuous woman.

Being a woman means being powerful and assertive, yet kind at the same time. It means being compassionate and vulnerable towards those we love in our lives without feeling weak for doing so. It means striving for our goals even in the face of adversity we may encounter along the way. A strong woman knows she has strength enough for the journey, but a woman of strength knows it is in the journey that she will become strong. You must love and care for yourself because that's when the best comes out. Self-empowerment means making a conscious decision to take charge of your destiny. It involves making positive choices, taking action to advance, and being confident in making and executing decisions. Self-empowered people understand their strengths and weaknesses and are motivated to learn and achieve. An inspiring woman is simply a woman who can fill someone with the desire or urge to do something worthwhile. Something that creates a better world. A woman of distinction appreciates life with everything it has got to offer.

A virtuous woman is expensive and has invested time, morals, principles, prayer, money, and hard work in herself. Her lover trusts her because she is all there is to be in a woman, a complete package, a woman with balance. She nurtures, loves, and cares. A good woman knows how to keep her unwanted emotions under control and handle things well. She also knows how to calm her man. It doesn't mean that she should agree to everything. But the important thing is to deal with disagreements to build a stable relationship. A lady models civility in how she treats others. She demonstrates respect, restraint, and personal responsibility in her appearance, behaviour, and communication. She is honourable and values and respects others. A lady is well-mannered and knows what is appropriate. So many unpleasant personalities fuel gossip; remember, when your tongue slips, it is hard to gain credibility. A sage woman is silent in the rage of anger. A discerning woman knows how to choose her words before it destroys her friendships.

Scripture Matthew 7: 7- 8: *"Ask, and it shall be given you; seek, and you*

shall find; knock, and it shall be opened unto you. For every one that asks receives, and he that seeks finds; and to him that knocks it shall be opened."

Simplistic truths… how often do we tap into it? Are we inspired by the galvanized effects it has? Are we putting this into action? Ultimately are you seeing those doors flying open in your path? To seek means to seek HIS ways fundamentally. We cannot lack integrity, and the whole nine yards, knock and expect the proverbial door to swing in our favour. If you seek, **align yourself to the North Star – Jesus, and He will unlock those doors**. A wise woman understands how to play the bat and ball. She is buoyed by her internal vector.

Truth decays in our society, homes, relationships, friendships, families, and workspaces. We have stood up for so much and changed the course of history, yet as women, we also tarnish the beauty and unravel it in mysterious ways. We let envy get in and ruin the plot. A smart woman discerns the baubles of life, she will understand how to value friendships. It is especially challenging for a woman to support and cheer another woman who appears to be more successful. Bitterness and envy rush to the surface. We covet what she has but have never walked in her shoes. You can use many adjectives to describe me, and success has been a palpable part of my journey, coupled with distress. I did not dwell in the latter state. Favour found me, and I have felt women look down their noses at me disdainfully.

I was prompted by the Holy Spirit to write a book, to help humanity. After my book was published, I experienced a new side of women and reached the status of international bestselling author. The contempt took a twist on steroids – wow! Ladies, life is not a competition. I supported and championed courses both financially and emotionally. Yet these women acted like I was invisible when my book launched, which was a success. My friends turned to foes because their personalities could not handle my success. This is our little pond, yet we want to reach for change on a global scale. Begin cleaning your heart; how can we fix the gender gap when we cannot stand on the same platform as another woman and champion her course? We may never get used to living next door to Alice or seeing her ride the success wave better than us. Ladies, our petulance is irksome. These stark realities are certainly correlated with the condition of our hearts. Kindness is free, sprinkle that stuff every day and everywhere. I relentlessly tried to maintain my modicum of inclusion. I gathered my offerings, unfilled cup, and talents and dashed out of the bustling arena. Do not dwell where you are not celebrated, encouraged, supported, honoured, and valued. Make room for each other until there is no place to hide. Do you celebrate phenomenal women in your world? Do you cultivate a no-competition zone – backstabbing, jealousy, or hate space? Do you nurture habits that confirm, I support you regardless of your circumstances? Is there energy that is worth bottling? If you are not excited about your friend's success, you are sadly not a friend. You do not need to push others to make a place in the sky; there is ample space for every woman to shine.

A symbolic gesture that is supposedly triumphant is our character of how we treat other women that are achieving goals. Instead, attitude is born out of desperation to disparage because we cannot attain the same achievements. Be a woman that dons that inclusive expression frequently in all life matters. When you step into the light, decide to be worthy of the limelight. The laconic mode of all our default characters should be constant self-awareness. Conduct comprehensive meta-analytic reviews that indicate your values and how you treat another woman. **Refrain from establishing conclusions without confirming evidence; an arbitrary influence will mould your patterns and character negatively**. How can we achieve success in a broader scope when we dwell in the domain of personal conflict? No woman should need your permission to succeed, and if she does SOAR without your support, it highlights the essence of woman camaraderie!

Women

Of

Distinction

Focused
Sincere
Kind
Compassionate
Achiever
Strong
Leader
Skilled
Creative
Emotional
Discerning
Observant
Innovative
Perfectly in Progress
Virtuous
Moral
Resourceful
Capable
Diligent
Disciplined
Vulnerable

84

Creating Your Legacy

"Your economic security does not lie in your job; it lies in your own power to produce – to think, to learn, to create, to adapt. That's true financial independence. It's not having wealth; it's having the power to produce wealth."
– Stephen Covey

How do you react to women that are more successful than you?

_____
_____
_____
_____

How do you respond to women who need your help?

_____
_____
_____
_____

In what ways are you virtuous?

_____
_____
_____
_____

Why do you empower yourself?

_____
_____
_____
_____
_____
_____
_____
_____
_____
_____

Personal Development Goals

_____
_____
_____
_____
_____
_____
_____
_____
_____
_____
_____
_____
_____
_____
_____
_____
_____
_____
_____
_____
_____
_____
_____
_____
_____
_____
_____
_____
_____
_____
_____
_____

Valid Productivity

"The effectiveness of productive effort, especially in industry, as measured in terms of the rate of output per unit of input" refers to the meaning of productivity as depicted in the dictionary. We have a plethora of insights on how to manage personal productivity. We are bombarded with the fundamentals of organising obligations, ambitions, and habits to competently and dependably complete what matters most.

Ryan Fuller, in Harvard Business Review: The Paradox of Workplace Productivity, *"defines productivity as value produced divided by resources (cost or time) required. This means that personal productivity is much more than just completing tasks; it's the value of the tasks you get done compared to the time and money you spend on them. To increase personal productivity, measuring how much you spend on your different tasks is essential to ensure it aligns with what's most important to you."* *"What's most important to you"* strikes a chord with me. Time, energy, resources, and outcome are all part of the equation. No matter how intelligently intentional you are about your productivity, it will form a base of brouhaha if it is vain and shallow. You may have ticked off the stereotype checkboxes. *"It's the value of the tasks you get done"* strikes a greater chord. Can you sense the advantage of your existence from just ticking off boxes? Come to the corporate round table to find versions of your humble self and birth authentic productivity.

In January 2021, the world woke up to the news that New Zealand's Prime Minister, Jacinda Arden, genuinely reflected on her productivity and decided to resign. *"I no longer have enough in the tank to do it justice."* These were the words from Jacinda Ardern, New Zealand's youngest Prime Minister in 150 years, announcing her decision to resign on 7 February 2021. *"I'm a politician who is first and foremost a human,"* Ardern said of the announcement, explaining that after six *"challenging"* years, she felt she would be doing a *"disservice to New Zealand"* if she continued in the job.

In 2019, Ardern spoke with LinkedIn News. Here are some takeaways:

On balance: *"Pick something important to you and be disciplined about that one thing."*

On allyship in politics: *"The idea of supportive environments and politics doesn't always seem like it goes together. In every workplace, we should create environments where we look out for one another."*

Advice for women entering the workforce: *"There are times when things will get tough. Always back yourself."*

On flexibility in the workplace: *"We're not beings who exist over here in compartments at work and over here in life… we need to keep making sure we're creating environments where people can juggle those responsibilities."*

How important is it for **YOU** to speak up about your well-being, the welfare of others, and where humanity is heading? How do you assess what you have *"in the tank?"* What changes will you make to your productivity? Are you content with the status quo of just ticking the boxes and remaining on your path? What is a human-first approach to you? What insights are you leaving the world with while you are being productive? You need to chew on your contemplating pen and establish what your tentative outline is and what partially hems you in. We have a stubborn populous and carnal incontinence regarding the truth about productivity. We all boast the status of being busy and achieving. What are we achieving? Does your productivity shrink the platform of meaningful ascent?

This self-examination may be gleefully brutalising, but you must enhance your objectives.

Step away from just ticking boxes and regarding yourself as productive. Escape appropriately contrite with new zeal to focus on what makes our world productive. Put your hand at the helm and make it matter with the time, effort, and resources you use. Become acutely aware of how YOUR PRODUCTIVITY can change the narrative. There exists a form of asymmetry in relation to accommodating approaches and proposals. Understanding that lives are derailed. Many still live in a bubble due to a noteworthy intellectual and cultural gap. Compassion for all forms of discrimination experienced globally requires acknowledgment and rectification. Zooming into the extensive posture of the spectrum from responsibilities to scrutiny. Mandating the process to include but not limited to, this schemer of targeted solutions can form the justification for change:

Impartial collaboration – how productive are you about this?

A plan to decline the systemic discrimination culture – What creativity have you sparked with this?

Rational destabilisation of inhumane laws – output is the real intelligence.

Conviction of acts of cruelty – efficiency tells the story.

Conscious awareness of negative culture and behaviour – yield with action

Insight to bias – the ostrich syndrome is not productive.

Custodianship clause – what part do you play in the equation?

Decolonisation legislature – how do you close the gap regarding psychological aspects of the colonial experience?

Authentic liberation – where do you stand?

Call out and address community, society, national, and international rhetoric – how are you doing that now?

The practice of genuine UBUNTU – act like you mean it.

Create a global Royal Commission Standard of guiding principles – vital productivity.

Regardless of citizenship, culture, or creed, every race should be factored into the ethics of a solution. An execution that spawns and generates variable manifestations of healing. Change the narrative from complacency and fleeting accountability. Create global industry standards for recognised practices, enforce Royal Commission standards, and introduce hefty penalties when actions are not challenged or changed after the problems are identified. Refrain from just ticking boxes. Comprehend, model, and action **PRODUCTIVITY IN YOUR SOLUTIONS**. Productivity is hyped. What makes a material difference is the quality that you produce. Was the effort valuable? *"Intelligence without ambition is a bird without wings."* – Salvador Dali. Productivity is not just using your time, money, and energy wisely. It is making a difference in what you produce.

What is authentic productivity to you? Plausibly persistent with your progressive patronage, assets aplenty, leader of the pack, flock tactics, still grappling with the sins of the past and the struggle to atone, honing in the vicissitudes of management styles, sitting in opulent silence, reunited with the surrendered mobile phone, or simply illustrating portraits of academic poise with hints of esteem. We are all fashioned differently. Dabble in seeking what gives vital productivity meaning to you, then live by it. Breathe it, and permit it to fashion you and the world in prominent ways.

"Whatever you do, do it well. For when you go to the grave, there will be no work or planning or knowledge or wisdom." – Ecclesiastes 9:10. This scripture offers insight into living an uncut life.

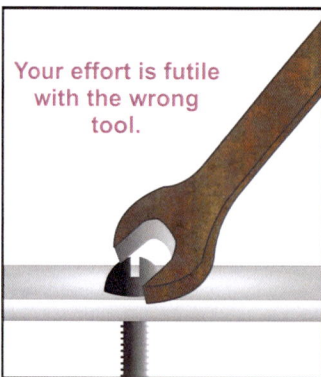

Your effort is futile with the wrong tool.

Substantiating your life with meaningful pursuit. Keep yourself busy with activity – an activity that makes a material difference. Take accountability for what is entrusted to you as a custodian. Why bother to do anything in an average way? If it is worth doing, then do it with excellence. Never get trapped in a culture of entitlement, demanding a reward to match your effort. Reward yourself by living to your highest values. You cannot be productive at anything when you are not equipped with the right tools. Mindset, ambition, knowledge, and wisdom are the greatest tools.

Creating Your Legacy

"It can be a challenge, but my legacy, at least for the people who came before me, is you don›t run from challenges because that›s more comfortable and convenient." – Bryan Stevenson

What is vital productivity to you?

_____
_____
_____
_____

What do you fill your tank up with to do justice in your work or life?

_____
_____
_____
_____

How can you improve to doing what you do well?

_____
_____
_____
_____

Do you have the right tools for vital productivity?

_____
_____
_____
_____
_____
_____
_____
_____
_____
_____

Personal Development Goals

_____

_____

_____

_____

_____

_____

_____

_____

_____

_____

_____

_____

_____

_____

_____

_____

_____

_____

_____

_____

_____

_____

_____

_____

_____

_____

_____

_____

_____

_____

_____

_____

_____

_____

_____

_____

Character Building

With reference to Cambridge dictionary character building means *helping* to make someone *emotionally stronger, more independent, and better* at *dealing* with *problems.* Reports have reflected that youth should be taught a variety of character-building skills such as having self-respect and respect for others, have you noticed any return on this investment? Have you taken notice of the calibre of adults that the world churns out? Has society blossomed with class? The reality of the characters that make the world spin is not a cocktail of surprises. Building character is no different from constructing a building – both require a firm foundation. Understanding what forms your secure foundation that improves upon your mental and moral characteristics is the onset.

Adversity is not always character-forming. Some people glean nothing in this season of life. Life does present us with moral dilemmas. We have all been thrust into situations where our professional responsibilities unexpectedly come into conflict with our deepest values. It is a red flag, for example, when you are in a financial crisis, or greed compels you to act in compromising ways. It denotes that your character is of the calibre that is weak and bargaining. Ambition does not correlate to automatic success; a remarkable character does. Even after you have traversed the well-worn path, your character makes you stand out from the crowd. Money shouts but wealth whispers… character paints a vista with clarity. The story of two teardrops floating down the river of life. One teardrop said to the other, "Who are you?" The other replied, "I'm a teardrop from a girl who loved and lost a man. Who are you?" The first one answered, "I'm a teardrop from the girl who got him." Always remember that your choices define your character, and your character creates your story – your story tangibly affects others.

I was strapped in on an international flight for a long haul, flicking through the entertainment channel to find something to occupy my time, I stumbled upon this movie. *"The explosive family drama at the centre of Ridley Scott's House of Gucci is so over-the-top that it's reasonable to assume the film is the result of a very active imagination. In the film – the marriage of Patrizia Reggiani (Lady Gaga) and Maurizio Gucci (Adam Driver) implodes as the family business, the House of Gucci, begins to crumble under the pressure of in-fighting and cultural shifts, culminating in the shocking murder of Maurizio. But in the case of House of Gucci, the truth is truly stranger than fiction. The film was adapted from journalist Sara Gay Forden's 2001 nonfiction book of the same name, which chronicled the sensational real-life story of the fabulously wealthy Gucci family's rise and fall as one of fashion's most prominent dynasties. The tale, which includes Succession-esque rivalries between family members, multiple lawsuits, tax evasion, incarceration and, of course, murder, provided ample creative fodder for Scott and screenwriters Roberto Bentivegna and Becky Johnston."*

Once the movie concluded, sleep eluded me. I was amplifying the need for robust character-building in my train of thought. What a powerhouse brand, and it all came down crumbling. A wife murders her husband – character served on a platter; why wait for justice to mirror who you are when your deeds do? Perhaps you are not a character that takes a knife to a gunfight. You have toiled to be a fabric of finer essence and stay off the fighting patch. You have gleaned when to walk away and let vengeance find its course – authentic character. You have discovered that marriage is not combat to flex your memory and repartee – a trustworthy character. You formulate your character in defining moments when you pledge your irreversible choice of action that profiles your individual and qualified identities. You divulge something new about yourself and others because defining moments uncover something that has been hidden or crystallize something that has been only partially known. You test yourself to unravel whether you will live up to your ideals or only pay them lip service.

How do you combine principle with practicality? Do you ponder before you set your character in motion? Many suffer from ethical myopia because their character was conditioned and fashioned by: variations in upbringing, faith, culture, training, personal forte, individual grit, and a moral force that dwells within them. The hallmark of character often reveals with precision when the stakes are high, and you put your significance first. Do you have a hidden agenda, or does a moral force guide you? A person struggling with the pecking order is evasive on details; how they treat those offering no benefits reveals character. Even the way you treat an animal reveals elements of your core character. Defining moments force you to seek a balance between your reality and morality – this is where the rubber hits the road, and your character comes home to roost.

German philosopher Friedrich Nietzsche wrote, *"I believe it is precisely through the presence of opposites and the feelings they occasion that the great man—the bow with great tension—develops."* Crucial moments bring those *'opposites'* and *'feelings'* organised into brilliant focus. The quest to balance your agenda and moral force presents a cluttered reality. Any situation is a prospect for exceptional action and personal evolution. Taking steps to build your character is no simple feat. Society pays attention to those who do what is correct rather than what is comfortable. The fact is that some people are attractive regardless of how they look. Your face and body are not the only reflections of your objective features; your emotions, attitude, values, and character also define the tapestry of your appealing beauty.

When a person is dishonest, disloyal, and untruthful, the negativity they carry not only masks their outer beauty but also the beauty of the soul. This is one of the reasons why we feel uneasy around certain people. When a person is genuine and truthful, the soul starts to reflect, and they even start to look attractive physically. Woefully, in the reality of the Gucci story, the husband felt an undercurrent of his wife's character and distanced himself – it cost him his life because he underestimated her character. When you keep your heart clear and your intentions genuine, your soul will reflect accordingly, your relationships will thrive in harmony, and you will look more beautiful.

Character building is an effort that most certainly pays dividends. Some illustrate examples include:

- **Be humble:** Humility is the beginning of wisdom. To build your character, you must be open to new ways.

- **Live out your principles and values:** Do the right thing. It will create a steadfast character.

- **Be intentional:** Integrity does not happen by chance. Creating a habit of positive values produces excellent character.

- **Practice self-discipline:** Great character has the acumen to do what is right over what is easy.

- **Be accountable:** Surround yourself with people who have high expectations. Permit others to push you to a robust character.

- **Discipline:** Character building requires discipline where an individual makes sacrifices.

- **Risk-taking:** Calculated risk-taking is fundamental to character building.

- **Debate:** The experience of arguing and trying to persuade others builds admirable character traits such as tolerance for disagreement and personal resilience.

- **Trust and honour:** These are critical to character building; you must build a culture to showcase your trust and honour.

- **Personal reflection**: Reflection also converts your character. Become intentional to form periods of quiet personal reflection.

- **Culture:** Immersion in morals, standards, outlooks, language, history, traditions, art, fictional myths, folklore, entertainment, and rites of passage of cultures influence character.

- **Toil:** Modern society seeks to eliminate toil; however, devoting your full attention to humble work can be character-building.

What makes a person consciously murder a loved one? No doubt it is a Pandora's box. Rest assured, character is the fundamental driving force to pull the trigger or not. Have you intentionally fashioned your character? Do you know if you would react or respond in a moment of plight? The sky may seem far, but it is not beyond reach. You can achieve your desired character one day at a time, a straightforward choice at a time. Ego and pride are strands of your character as well. The more you embroil these emotions into your character, the more they will steal the narrative of your life. They will cost you everything and leave you with nothing. Character building is a paramount reckoning in life… dare to indulge and taste the sweetness or defy and tolerate the brunt!

If you do not proactively build your character then external forces will compel you to develop new skills.
Photograph:
Melbourne, Australia
2022

Creating Your Legacy

"The mediocre teacher tells. The good teacher explains. The superior teacher demonstrates. The great teacher inspires." – William Arthur Ward

How are you accountable?

_____
_____
_____
_____

What's on your moral agenda?

_____
_____
_____
_____

In what ways does your character shine?

_____
_____
_____
_____

How do you challenge dysfunction in your character?

_____
_____
_____
_____
_____
_____
_____
_____
_____
_____

Personal Development Goals

_____
_____
_____
_____
_____
_____
_____
_____
_____
_____
_____
_____
_____
_____
_____
_____
_____
_____
_____
_____
_____
_____
_____
_____
_____
_____
_____
_____
_____
_____
_____
_____

Influential Finesse

When a warthog sees a lion every cell in its brain sends a chain reaction to shut off other parts of the system such as digestion, sound, smell or sex and all energy is focused on running from the lion, this is anxiety in motion. No time to stop and ponder other facets of life when your life is threatened. How often do you slip into your ultimate mould to survive when catastrophe strikes? I believe the abundance of our hearts or our unadvertised values comes to the surface in moments like this. We exhibit influential prowls and demonstrate our finesse even in the chaos model.

Recently, I saw this palpably modelled to me by a woman who exhibited influential finesse in her stride. I salute a woman of this calibre. How we manage ourselves, our personal lives, and our families gives us the same brush and canvas to paint in our corporate portfolio. Just like the warthog, we go into a lock and survival mode. Do you paint a picture of panache when exhibiting your influential finesse to the world?

After six years in a coma, German player Schumacher wakes up and recognises his wife. His wife spent most of her money on treating her husband until bankruptcy. Despite the big money Schumacher had earned from his Formula 1 income as he dominated the race for years and all his sponsorship and contracts, all the money was spent. There was the loss of hope for his recovery until he woke up one day, and the first person he got to know was his wife, this woman who stayed by his side and did not abandon him for six years.

Society is passionate about marrying and dating financially stable partners, disregarding the focus on mental, emotional, superior vigour and grit in a crisis. Ignoring what real influential finesse comes with the package that wishes to place your ring as a final resting place. To manage the external corporate domain, you must first master managing your personal sphere. When you learn to identify and manage the small, often hard microelements, you automatically learn how to manage this in every facet of life. It will come naturally like it does for you to talk. Schumacher's wife displayed her influential finesse to the world when catastrophe threatened her normal life.

Do not be scared to be associated with a robust woman. There will come a day when she will exempla to you in profound ways even while she is in her valley of despair. You can have a lifetime of experience or live every day making the same mistakes as day one. The distinct difference between age and maturity is when doing the same old thing for 50 years and getting the same results. Whatever page you are on, glamorous and sophisticated, not just carrying the scars but creating some of them, showcasing the Freudian slip of the tongue, displaying public tears for private pain, and holding onto a private admiration. You are already a living marketing platform – your character is a brand. The ultimate question is, what are you advertising to yourself, to your inner circle, and to your corporate gorillas?

What matters to you more than looking after your best worker? Is your style built on emotions or sheer profits and favouritism? Victims and bullies walk, live, and work among us. Do not just kick the can down the road, bring your influential finesse to the table every day. Finesse allows trailblazers to steer tricky situations, such as office politics, and intense clashes, the prerequisite to be frank to those higher on the hierarchy. Finesse has fundamental components: the power of self-awareness, the ability to read the situation and stakeholders, the skill to foresee the impact, the aptitude to convey a measured presence, the talent to differ with the issue, not the organization or person, a knack to be a mirror to help people adjust, capability to get tasks done through others. When strategically honed in to focus only on results, you can reduce your ability to reveal finesse.

If Schumacher's wife had focused on her depleting finances, then perhaps the narrative would have been different for both her and her husband. This woman models to us her influential finesse just like the warthog chased by a lion – she slips into what comes naturally. The values that she wants to live by, the promises that she made, and the vows that she took. Your ability to influence others begins with the vision in the mirror. The character that you are behind closed doors will influence people in the arena. Influencing others is essential, but it's more than just giving commands. A brighter picture is painted when you stimulate, encourage, and inspire others toward a common goal.

Influential finesse radiates the beautiful resonance of your character in or out of Zoom meetings, spattering it all spontaneously, whether disorganized, marvellous, outstanding, or unattractive. To be truly effective – in good times and in times of great challenge – leaders must master the ability to influence others. By definition, influence is the ability to affect the behaviour of others in a particular direction, leveraging key strategies that include, associate, and stimulate others. Significant spearheads know that by promoting themselves authentically, for the right reasons, they can cut through the information that bombards us all each day. Building and maintaining a fountain of trust is essential for leading. Without trust, leaders may be able to force people to comply, but they will never tap the full commitment, capabilities, and creativity the group can offer. Leveraging these assets is invaluable when tackling tough challenges or making strategic changes, so trust is vital. I guess Schumacher knew exactly who he wanted on his team, especially when the chips were down, and he could not fend for himself.

Everyone reaching for that mountain recognizes and cultivates the power of networks. Organizations are progressively dynamic. They transform in size and shape over time. Influential leaders recognize that their networks must also be dynamic, and they continually grow and strengthen their networks. They are strategic about choosing how and when to tap into this network. The essence of a relationship or marriage morphs into different seasons as well. I am certain that Schumacher's wife could not be at his side for six consecutive years championing his recovery without a network to sustain her. Every situation or project needs silent builders to get the job done.

Work until you no longer have to introduce yourself, especially when your influential finesse precedes your reputation. May you excursion enthusiastically but always towards those shards and darts of light that clarify the obscurity with your ultimate influence, and may you close the gap to purposeless gestures with your loud acts of finesse. Success may be in humble but profound disciplines practised every day for six years until boom – a result presents. When your marriage or organisation has lethal superstars, the sophistication of ethos is lost. We are presented with a malfunctioning incentive system. A healthy marriage or organisation will default to duties of care that go above and beyond any financial gain, routine, or advancement. It speaks straight from the heart, with no hidden agendas.

Exempla

Stimulate

Ethos

Influential Finesse

Creating Your Legacy

"The purpose of life is not to be happy. It is to be useful, to be honourable, to be compassionate, to have it make some difference that you have lived and lived well." – Ralph Waldo Emerson

In what ways do you influence the world?

_____
_____
_____
_____

What elements of life impacts you?

_____
_____
_____
_____

How have you become a spearhead to create influential finesse?

_____
_____
_____
_____

When did you display virtue and integrity with the mundane aspects of life?

_____
_____
_____
_____
_____
_____
_____
_____
_____
_____

Personal Development Goals

_____
_____
_____
_____
_____
_____
_____
_____
_____
_____
_____
_____
_____
_____
_____
_____
_____
_____
_____
_____
_____
_____
_____
_____
_____
_____
_____
_____
_____
_____
_____
_____

Legacy

Even if the majority are on a path, this does not dictate that you must follow suit. It takes an abundance of pluck, audacity, and forte to refuse to follow the herd. You must garner greater vigour to wear a brave face and generate your path. Construct an utterly crystal-clear vision that will unravel your legacy in a vista that no one can miss, not even the future generation. Style up some super goals + stellar daily action steps that will set the pace for the birth of your legacy. Everything you require is already inside of you. Do not wait for others to kindle your fire. You have your spark; ignite it. Proactively produce direction to your life; if not, the lack of direction will take over the narrative, determine your purpose, and serve up a default legacy – you will be responsible for the birth of this legacy.

"If you want the rainbow, you've gotta put up with the rain." – Dolly Parton. When was the last time you did something for the first time? Your decisions determine your destiny and legacy, fear to create, and refusal to plunge into. The quality of your choices and decisions sets the scene. How worthwhile is your legacy? Are you building something valuable? The most meaningful legacy aligns with your core principles and reveals your authentic character; it spills the abundance of your heart into the world. Fear and anxiety are normal emotions necessary for survival, but never let them derail your legacy. The riddle of life is always tantalising, and the scope is nothing short of soul-shaping. The modern world is full of false dichotomies. Reason and revelation, fact and value, your choice is to choose truth over technicality or figment. Do not stop trying because the system or schemes have conditioned you to stop trying.

If you want your life to be different and live it on purpose, then you must intentionally define and implement your goals. No one gets to the top of a mountain accidentally. Become purposely accountable. Find friends and family members you trust and share your goals with them. Permit them to hold you accountable. Alternatively, hire a coach(es) to help you achieve your goals and stay focussed. Design your personal development. Growth does not happen automatically. Your growth in age will be automatic, but you have to be intentional about developing the real you – your mind. You must invest in changing the way you think because nothing changes until the way you think changes.

Evaluate your relationships. Your relationships are always a reflection of where you are headed in life. You are the sum total of the five people you spend the most time with. So, look at your close friends. Do they look like where you want to be? If not, it's time to change your circle of friends or influence. A regular analysis is an excellent opportunity to purge toxic and mediocre people from your life. Make peace with the past. Your past does not equate to your future – it only does if you do not take strategic action. Permit bygone to be bygone. Refrain from flirting with your past, and all it represents. Bury your past. Divorce yourself from resentment, offence, and unforgiveness. Be purposeful about love, peace, joy, hope, and gratitude. Ask God for guidance. It will guarantee the tone for a paradigm shift in your life. Your body, soul, and mind will align in accordance. Leave no stone unturned to discover your purpose, values, and the legacy you want to create.

Here are some prompts to help you define your goals and character to create your desired legacy. You can go as deep and comprehensive as you prefer. Use an additional book if you require to create additional notes.

Goals and Character Building for Creating a Legacy		
PHYSICAL **How does your endurance and strength influence your legacy?**		
SPIRITUAL **What obligations, values, beliefs, and accetpances must you create to establish your legacy?**		
BEHAVIOURAL **What behaviours do you prefer to stop, reduce, start, or continue to fashion your legacy?**		
COGNITIVE **What thoughts and mindset would you like to change or enhance to imporove your future legacy?**		

Goals and Character Building for Creating a Legacy

EMOTIONAL What emotions or feelings would you like to reduce or harness to fashion your legacy?		
FINANCIAL What financial goals would you prefer to implement to style your legacy?		
FAMILY How do you prefer to strenghten or eradicate family bonds that will champion your legacy?		
CONTRIBUTION What will your contribution to life be?		
FUNERAL What would you prefer to be said during this chapter?		
TOMBSTONE What words would you like etched on your tombstone?		

Goals and Character Building for Creating a Legacy		
ACCEPTANCE What do you need to accept about yourself and what do you need to change?		

Life is astonishing. Sometimes it is dreadful. Sandwiched with the astonishing and dreadful is the serving of familiar, monotonous, and regular. Relish the astonishing, build your forte, and prepare for the next season. Learn to dance, respite, sing, and unwind when the familiar, monotonous, and regular visits. Abundant life has a balance of restoration and catastrophe. Herein, you discover how to live authentically and discover what and why a legacy is meaningful to you. You will begin to comprehend how distress manufactures stamina, and your determination produces character, and character produces hope. Hope will give you the zeal to create a legacy. The future is not something you propose. The future is something you design. Never remain trapped in the suffering of the familiar instead of seeking a better future. Excuses make today comfortable but tomorrow difficult. Discipline makes today tough but tomorrow much more tender.

You can tolerate it; perhaps you are malfunctioning and even living in hardship. You can still survive and move forward to a place where you will thrive because tomorrow is a new beginning. Misfortune is not the opposite of victory; disappointment is part of success. Life bestows ample thrills and magnificence – have you got the potential to harness this and create an extraordinary life? In the Bible, we read Gideon was found in a hole. Joseph was in prison. Daniel was banished to a lion's den. If you ever feel untrained, remember these men created a legacy that is etched in history, and I am certain they did not wake up feeling qualified. Rest assured that life will test you every single day, not to punish you but to train you. Your distinguished life is built by design.

Creating a legacy takes time. It's crucial to start today. What is your exceptional influence on the world? Nelson Mandela, Oprah Winfrey, Thomas Edison, and Martin Luther King Jr contributed. Not all of us can fill these prominent shoe examples. However, you are unique and can leave your flavour to linger in the world. Creating a succession plan for unforeseen circumstances ensures your legacy lives on. The indolent reap dire consequences. Foster the courage to become imperturbable in the waves of change and curve balls that come your way. Stay tuned to your mission, purpose, and legacy, and avoid desultory behaviour every time you hit a bump. "What you leave behind is not what is engraved in stone monuments, but what is woven into the lives of others." – Pericles

Creating Your Legacy

"I don't want to end up simply having visited this world." – Mary Oliver

What was the most unforeseen thing you have discovered about yourself?

_____

_____

_____

_____

What habits do you prefer to stop?

_____

_____

_____

_____

What aspects of your life you prefer to improve?

_____

_____

_____

_____

List the new things that you prefer to incorporate into your life.

_____

_____

_____

_____

Identify and address how you will overcome any challenge that may present.

_____

_____

_____

_____

_____

_____

_____

Personal Development Goals

Final Words

Life continually formulates an entrance to influence, it offers **YOU** a tabula rasa every morning. You can create a life and voice like audible incense, put the pedal to the metal. There will always be a perpetual gap between where you are and where you want to be, which may feel like an abyss. Take courage that you are aware of the gaping gap. Put on your chutzpah and unravel it. Your legacy and destiny will stand the test of time when you manage the moments you feel defeated with audacity. How do you contour your character when in pain, what influences every season of your life regardless of circumstances, and how do you manage the narration of your history? Remember never to lose focus of your vision to keep your legacy alive. Redefine your formula and goals if you have to.

Fear is debilitating; it makes you concerned about doing something incorrect, appearing unwise, or not meeting expectations. Psychologists have confirmed that generating approach goals, or positively reframing avoidance goals, benefits wellbeing. When you dread a tough task and expect it to be difficult and unpleasant, you may unconsciously set goals around what you do not want to happen rather than what you do want. Reframe your avoidance goals. Place your emphasis on learning. The crumbs will never fall where you desire. When you comprehend that reality at the onset, you can squeeze the most value out of the experience, no matter the outcome.

Enthusiasm is brief; instead, cultivate obedience and self-proficiency. Become adept at managing your life in both the current and future state. Be aware of those who steal your passion and teach you with their desire. This life is yours. Take the power to choose what you want to do and do it well. Take the authority to control your own life. You need to find your enthusiasm if you want to succeed in building a legacy. Your zeal may not be as delightful as a braai in a boardroom meeting. Effort and indoctrination will help you develop curiosity, engaging in proper self-evaluation, self-reflection, or self-examination to seek the facts. The truth is about your life, where you want it to be, and what you want to leave behind when the final curtain is drawn. Weed out the quotidian and dig deep for the gems of your life. Leave a resplendent heirloom for future generations.

Plant the seeds of your wildest dreams and watch them grow into reality. Never allow a struggle to turn your sky into a ceiling. You must always believe there is a way. Life is a journey with problems to resolve and lessons to glean, but most of all, experiences to appreciate. Life allows everyone to leave an impeccable remnant that creates a lasting window to your audacious life. An African proverb – *"A wise man fills his brain before emptying his mouth."* Take your cue from this profound wisdom and fill your life before you exit. Growth is messy, ugly, and painful. Still, your legacy and destiny mandate that you heal, address those bad habits, become accountable, and treat those traumas, do not leave an unhealthy mess for someone else to declutter.

Life will always compete for your priorities. The onus is upon you to organise both your faculties and primacies. When television was presented, society forgot how to prioritise books. Once the wheel was invented and the innovations progressed, humanity overlooked how important walking is. Steve Jobs revolutionised our world with the astounding invention of the smartphone, this affords us connection and opportunities at our fingertips, yet we are so disconnected and constantly yearning. We have advanced to using voice narration and woefully forgot how to write handwritten letters and spell appropriately. When the air-conditioner made its debut, we forgot how to venture out beneath the shade of a lush tree to enjoy the cool organic breeze. Children believe money is waiting for you at the automatic teller machine – all you have to do is enter your number. The joys of instant messaging have corrupted our level of patience and authentic conversations.

What percentage of time do you spend with your loved ones? What proportion of people you are connected to on social media are your friends? How much do you own from your combined assets compared to what you owe to the bank? How often do you use all the electronic gadgets in your home? What proportion of functionality do you use on your phone, television, car, oven, or laptop? What proportion of space do you constructively use in your home? What ratio of clothes do you proactively wear in your wardrobe? Do your answers tell a story that puts you in a rat race? The pertinent question is why? Only you can unravel what's important to you and what you prioritise – this will set the scene for the foundation of your legacy.

Sophistication in vuja de (something familiar) will always rob you of a fresh view. Why do you feel the need to be noosed to something recognisable? Even if you are grappling with a phobia, ambivalence, and self-doubt, harness spades of confidence to seek what legacy you want to build. Become passionate about specializing in creative forecasting and looking within. Refrain from guilt for unrefined prose and actions that emerge from your heart. Never get caught in a maze without a sense of direction. Ultimately crafting a legacy demands formulation, time, and commitment. The fundamental message for those interested in leaving a legacy is that construction should start immediately. Remember that actions manufacture legacies, not desires. *"In a gentle way, you can shake the world."* – Mahatma Gandhi.

Conscious pathway to legacy

The actions you take today will impact your loved ones, the future you construct, and the legacy you leave behind. Life will afford you ample creative fodder, what are you going to do with it? Are you lightning without warning? Even if the cape is not part of your daily apparel, you can be innovative, leaving gentle fingerprints on many lives. When you own your story, then you can write the ending. We have all been dying since birth. It's a condition that defines living. You can follow an espoused path to both your journey and destination. Become a captain of your faith, not a victim of your impulse. Do not fret because you have not started to live abundantly with purpose. Obama retired at 55, and Trump started at 70 – as US president. You have your time zone to bloom. Become strategic about your perception, vigour, obligation, efficiency, effect, and audacity. Each calamity and challenge that you face plays an integral part in the process of unfolding your legacy.

Research indicates that the ageing process is accelerated when people retire. Most people die eighteen months after retirement. Sadly, this is the time they have allocated to creating a legacy and living life to the fullest. Most have health, physical, and mental challenges at this stage. A vitalized life begins sooner rather than later. Prioritise and organise your life now and not when you retire. Identify what you value and prioritise it now. Find the magnificence of your routine now as it feeds your destiny. Do not build a life by default filled with mediocrity, deterioration, and randomness. The truth does not like to be questioned, and lies do not like to be challenged. To establish a legacy, you must question and challenge both – your lies convey as much as your truth. Break away from rose-tinted obsessions.

When the fantasy of life subsides, which it always does, where will you be left standing? Do you genuinely want to exit without a legacy? Your character is revealed slowly or swiftly by what you leave behind. Do not get trapped in a confused culture until it is too late. Trace your scared perception of reality and live it long after you are gone. Your mind's attic will still be accessible to the world. Discipline, in essence, is the consistency of action – steadiness with values, reliability with long-term goals, dependability with performance, established morals, staunchness in technique, and loyalty to time. These are the fundamental pillars for creating a legacy. Your lifespan is finite, but your legacy is infinite.

Legacy Plan Checklist

Some of us do not care what happens after death, and we already live aimless and uneventful lives. Have you asked yourself why you don't care about legacy and what you leave behind? Perhaps you may feel that you attained nothing in life. You do not have to explain or defend your journey or misfortunes. Rest assured, you can still leave your mark on the world and your family. Guide the younger generation with your wisdom and lived experience. Society will remember how you live more than the details of your achievements. Share the family traditions and stories with your children. Communicate authentically and share your failings as well as your triumphs. A legacy that speaks of transparency and an open spirit is a legacy that will benefit many generations. Some joke-smith pulls down the celestial ladder behind them, are you doing this consciously or unconsciously? Bring your latent talents to the fore with significant altruistic motivation to align.

We each live a story. The best stories are grounded in timeless values and commitments and are certainly bigger than we are. Appreciate confidence in human intuition. Live a story that lasts an eternity. Most people remember presence more than they remember presents. Commit enough to yourself that your legacy is that you loved enough to be there. Don't just be the perennial planner; speak about your vision after you have departed from this life. Share with your loved ones what kind of lives you would like them to live, even after you are deceased. I have no children; my legacy is etched in the books I created to help humanity. These books will stand the test of time and speak to readers long after I have departed. My legacy is created in the strands of lives that I touched and changed. Spring paints the landscape with many colours. What is your life painting? Do not allow the seasons of life to ruin your day; rule the day and your life.

What will your legacy be? What will live on after you are absent? Live your best life by creating a legacy you can be proud of. The more I ponder about my legacy, the greater my discernment and passion are to live my legacy now. While leaving a legacy is significant, it is not as imperative as living your legacy. I live with no neglect, I make the most of each day, I value each person and opportunity, I am certain about what my life stands for, I know precisely how the world is a better place via my influence, and I will continue to make contributions that will reap dividends beyond myself, I have confirmations of the lives that I have touched and changed, others will glean from my lived experience, and I understand that I was born to serve not just to be served.

Be comfortable in your skin. Know precisely who you are – a precious relic. There is merit in humanity appreciating my purpose while I am alive rather than when I am pushing daisies. However, death will not cease my cause, my passions and pursuits will thrive even after I am decayed... my legacy will continue my vision by:

- The expertise and knowledge I contributed to my profession
- The numerous books that I have written
- The people that I have helped around the world
- The awards that I have received
- The awards that I have created for people to benefit from my scholarship
- The inheritance that I have left behind for descendants
- My contribution to charity .
- Documenting family recipes
- Facilitating family traditions
- Obliging as a global role model
- Conduit to pass down family heirloom
- Global mentor
- International ambassador
- Volunteer on several platforms
- Impacting and shaping non-profit organization
- Partnerships with non-profit organization
- Podcasts
- Radio Interviews
- Magazine cover features
- Blogs

Here is a checklist for you to start planning and implementing your legacy:

Task	Action	Status
Determine what legacy you prefere to establish		
Begin with action steps today		
Streamline your life and focus on the essentials		
Define the impact you prefer to have on: ♦ Yourself ♦ Family ♦ Humanity		
Remember integrity will outlive you, do the right thing, especially when no one is watching you		
Be realistic with: ♦ Time ♦ Resources ♦ Skills		

Task	Action	Status
Align with your core values		
Establish both your micro and macro goals		

In addition, it is important to recognize barriers to building a legacy. A number of factors that can act as legacy blockers include:

Task	Action	Status
Lack of motivation		
Coerced to crafting the life others desire for you		
Bound by emotions of animosity, resentment, and anxiety		
Trapped in the perpetual cycle of consumerism		
Competing priorities		

Task	Action	Status
Always classifying stuff as emergencies		
Refusing to break away from the comfort blanket		
Lack of planning		
Always shelving things		
Misconception that you have enough time		
Pessimism creating a philosophy that it will not add value		
Levels of consciousness determine bottlenecks: Indirectly by you Directly by you To you		

As beautiful as the personality that she borrows from history, Cornelia Arnolda Johanna Corrie Ten Boom (15 April 1892 – 15 April 1983) was a Dutch watchmaker and later a Christian writer and public speaker, who worked with her father, Casper ten Boom, her sister Betsie ten Boom, and other family members to help many Jewish people escape from the Nazis during the Holocaust in World War II by hiding them in her home. They were caught, and she was arrested and sent to the Ravensbrück concentration camp. Her most famous book, *The Hiding Place*, is a biography that recounts the story of her family's efforts and how she found and shared hope in God while she was imprisoned at the concentration camp. Humanity can be dissected into men, women, and Corrie Ten Boom, what a sensational legacy she has left, gone but not forgotten. Her impeccable example lives on and continues to inspire.

Support and champion the course come what may. A covenant of trust is noted in the effort, efficiency, and dignity that manifests in your legacy. Humiliation could not be more complete when you allow the gaping wounds of life to derail this brief encounter of life and have nothing to show for it. Don't let your vanity get the better of you. However, on balance give meaning to the mystery before you start pushing daisies. We are all seeking relevance – be strategic. Just as the Spring rains bring revival to the soil, let your life replenish the thirst of your soul. Your life is a distinction of clout expending itself upon the picturesque – it is the vista that you will leave behind. Take all the time you need to mull over with some detachment what picture you will leave for the world. Will it be a silhouette in the arena from the 21st-century with a mindset from the Stone Age? Alternatively, will it be a picture that commends fertility and potential that pass through your hands creating cathedrals that are embraced and encouraged simultaneously? Do not get caught walking sedately in the twilight of your life. Let the cry from within arrest you.

The manner in which we trust each other in the absence of an established code of conduct tells the tale every single time, baby turtles' gender depends on the temperature of the sand that the eggs are laid in. The warmer the temperature this will revert to female turtles. Male hatchlings are required for the species to flourish. Humanity has a moral obligation to bring hope. Humanity cannot look the other way and presume the situation will resolve itself. *"In most species, gender is determined during fertilization. However, the sex of most turtles, alligators, and crocodiles is determined after fertilization. The temperature of the developing eggs is what decides whether the offspring will be male or female. This is called temperature-dependent sex determination, or TSD.*

Research shows that if a turtle's eggs incubate below 27.7° Celsius (81.86° Fahrenheit), the turtle hatchlings will be male. If the eggs incubate above 31° Celsius (88.8° Fahrenheit), however, the hatchlings will be female. Temperatures that fluctuate between the two extremes will produce a mix of male and female baby turtles. Researchers have also noted that the warmer the sand, the higher the ratio of female turtles. As the Earth experiences climate change, increased temperatures could result in skewed and even lethal incubation conditions, which would impact turtle species and other reptiles."

Research is taking a proactive approach to protect species and ensure future generations have a legacy, fauna, and flora that are intentional, not the default dregs leftover from lack of planning. Perish from mismanagement – you are a greater species and what you leave behind impacts the world on a larger scale. Your effort may be toilsome but it is valued and appreciated. It will forever change the ecosystem. Swearing of dreams begins with myriad calamities but that birth of legacy will stand the test of time. Life is not about finding, it's about creating, the decadence is unravelled in designing. *"The end of life is not to be happy, nor to achieve pleasure and avoid pain, but to do the will of God, come what may."* – Rev. Martin Luther King Jr. You can establish your legacy by working smarter, not harder.

Work Smarter Not Harder

Acknowledgements

I am delighted to publish another book it brings me great joy to acknowledge Loschinee Naiker the individual who have been instrumental in the birth of this book. She asked me to write for her blog and these articles motivated and inspired many readers, this took me on an incredible adventure to package this as a Legacy Playbook. Thank you for the opportunity to serve humanity in collaboration.

The principal rock, I want to express my deepest gratitude to my Husband – Dave. His unwavering love, creating the graphics, designing the cover, proof reading and taking responsibility for the types setting all at a great hourly rate – better than mate's rates. THANK YOU, I am utterly blessed to have you as a partner in crime.

I am indebted to my editor Cyrene for her expertise and dedication in bringing this book to life. Nicole Farrell for inscribing a heartfelt and inspiring foreword. Jennifer Ndlovu, Gai Carman, Patricia Mmatshetlha Mathabe and Rachel Biggar thank for writing acclaims to showcase this book.

To the countless mentors, teachers, and advisors who have shaped my acumen and thinking over the years, thank you for your wisdom and guidance. Your influence has had a profound impact on both my personal and professional growth.

I extend my thanks to the readers who have supported and embraced my previous works, motivating me to continue honing my craft. Your enthusiasm has been a driving force behind my desire to deliver my best efforts in this book.

Finally, I want to acknowledge all the individuals who may never read these words but have played a role in shaping the person I am today. Every encounter, every experience, and every moment of inspiration has left an imprint on my writing, and I am grateful for each one.

This book is the culmination of a dream I've carried with me for as long as I can remember, and it would not have been possible without the incredible people who surrounded me. Thank you all for being a part of this journey, and I hope that my words in this book resonate with you in some meaningful way.

About the Author

Kelly Markey is Founder and CEO of Markey Writing Academy. Winner of Top Executive of the Year 2023 – International Associations of Top Professionals. 2023 Woman Changing the World Award finalist and the NOBEL prize nominee. Kelly is a multi-time international bestselling author across many genres: non-fiction, motivational, self-help, memoir, corporate informational, professional technical writing, suicide prevention storytelling from the heart and journal. She is a well-sprouted philanthropist, rotary board forum, toastmaster member, Jay Shetty coach blogger, writer for Women's Biz Magazine, and leader and supporter for creating sustainable families and educating children in Uganda. Markey has a strong partnership with Zululand Lifeline South Africa to improve holistic care, a member of The Cancer Institute, Australia to support and champion research.

Undergraduate of the human spirit and soul, she is fluent in five languages, has vast overseas exposure, and travelled to more than 200 cities around the world. An accomplished keynote speaker, Markey is a strong advocate for equal opportunity and gender equality, she has worked tirelessly to help countless women realise their own strengths and equip them to become economically independent, Podcast Guest, Brand Ambassador, YouTube Guest, and in addition, she has graced magazines as cover features, radio stations, newspapers, and television.

Markey is a novice poet. She is an accomplished woman; Kelly is as great at golf as she is an avid reader. A fulfilled port elitist, a book club member, and a keen hiker. An eternal optimist and trailblazer. In addition, Markey has worked in concert with The Salvation Army nationally in Australia to design the first holistic model of aged care in the world. Kelly is a BRAND AMBASADOR for The Global Movement of HOPE.

Kelly Markey km

CEO Markey Writing Academy
Publisher
Writer's Consultant
Global Bestselling Author
Nobel Prize Nominee x 2
Top Executive 2023 - IAOTP
Women Changing the World Finalist
Brand Ambassador:
Global Movement of Hope
kellymarkey.com

Markey Writing Academy

Markey Writing Academy is an award-winning company providing an impeccable service to bring your expressive pen to life. Kelly's exclusive masterclass is streamlined to offer professional writers a pathway to obtain Nobel nominations and for novice authors to find their voice. Affording you impeccable publishing opportunities as well.

For further information visit www.kellymarkey.com

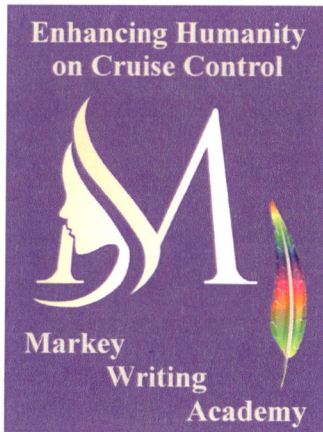

Other Books by Kelly Markey

- ◆ Don't Just Fly, SOAR
- ◆ Glean, Grow, Glow Journal
- ◆ Making Sage Decisions
- ◆ The Life of Jayandra

Reference

Preface

1. Reference to Machu Picchu, https://www.worldwildlife.org/blogs/good-nature-travel/posts/ten-interesting-facts-about-machu-picchu

2. Numbers 17:8, Zondervan, The Holy Bible, New International Translation (NIV), United States. Harper Collins, 1973.

3. Excerpt from the book Kelly Markey, Don't Just Fly, SOAR, Ultimate World Publishing, Australia, 2021.

4. Photograph, analysis, and specifications by Kelly Markey and CorelDRAW illustration by Dave Markey

Finding Opportunities Where the World Sees Obstacles

5. Reference to escape from Alcatraz prison, https://www.fbi.gov/history/famous-cases/alcatraz-escape

6. Graphics, analysis, and specifications by Kelly Markey and CorelDRAW illustration by Dave Markey

Don't Just Fly but Soar in Relationships

7. Luke 9:23, Zondervan, The Holy Bible, New International Translation (NIV), United States. Harper Collins, 1973.

8. Graphics, analysis, and specifications by Kelly Markey and CorelDRAW illustration by Dave Markey

Resilience

9. Resilience after devastation, https://www.usgs.gov/faqs/what-are-some-benefits-volcanic-eruptions

10. Psychological resilience, https://en.wikipedia.org/wiki/Psychological_resilience

11. Emotional and mental resilience, https://wellness.osu.edu/chief-wellness-officer/year-resilience

12. Reference to the 7C's in resilience, https://optionb.org/advice/the-7-cs-of-resilience-in-kids

13. Agatha Christie, https://powerofbooks.quora.com/https-ancienthistoryandmysterylovers-quora-com-Deeply-hurt-by-the-death-of-her-mother-thirty-five-year-old-Agatha-Chri

14. Graphics, analysis, and specifications by Kelly Markey and CorelDRAW illustration by Dave Markey

Confidence

15. Life of Harriet Tubman, https://en.wikipedia.org/wiki/Harriet_Tubman

16. Graphics, analysis, and specifications by Kelly Markey and CorelDRAW illustration by Dave Markey

Negative Self Talk

17. How the body replaces cells, https://www.discovery.com/science/Body-Really-Replace-Itself-Every-7-Years

18. Philippians 4:11–13, Zondervan, The Holy Bible, New International Translation (NIV), United States. Harper Collins, 1973.

19. Self-talk effects on athletes, https://www.ncbi.nlm.nih.gov/pmc/articles/PMC8947089/

20. Lyrics to the song Believer, https://genius.com/Guy-sebastian-believer-lyrics

21. Graphics, analysis, and specifications by Kelly Markey and CorelDRAW illustration by Dave Markey

Getting Unstuck

22. Perception of feeling stuck, https://www.ncbi.nlm.nih.gov/pmc/articles/PMC2743430/

23. John 4:4–30, Zondervan, The Holy Bible, New International Translation (NIV), United States. Harper Collins, 1973.

24. Photograph included with permission from Dave Markey

Forgiveness and Self Respect

25. Lady Macbeth syndrome, https://en.wikipedia.org/wiki/Lady_Macbeth_effect

26. Luke 17:3, Zondervan, The Holy Bible, New International Translation (NIV), United States. Harper Collins, 1973.

27. John 2:14- 15, Zondervan, The Holy Bible, New International Translation (NIV), United States. Harper Collins, 1973.

28. Graphics, analysis, and specifications by Kelly Markey and CorelDRAW illustration by Dave Markey

Setting Goals

29. Frozen Frog, https://www.livescience.com/32175-can-frogs-survive-being-frozen.html

30. Graphics, analysis, and specifications by Kelly Markey and CorelDRAW illustration by Dave Markey

Building Habits

31. It takes 66 days to form a habit, https://www.healthline.com/health/how-long-does-it-take-to-form-a-habit#tips-and-tricks

32. Reference to the book Psycho-Cybernetics, Dr. Maxwell Maltz, 1960, audible

33. Reference to the book, Daily Rituals: How Artists Work, 2017, Youtube

34. Sleeping on it, https://www.cdc.gov/niosh/emres/longhourstraining/napping.html

35. President Obama's habit to wear the same suit, https://www.fastcompany.com/3026265/always-wear-the-same-suit-obamas-presidential-productivity-secrets

36. Two hundred decisions about food per day, https://www.thecut.com/2016/05/you-will-make-200-decisions-about-food-today.html

37. Graphics, analysis, and specifications by Kelly Markey and CorelDRAW illustration by Dave Markey

Time Verses Energy

38. Load shedding in South Africa, https://en.wikipedia.org/wiki/South_African_energy_crisis

39. Harvard business review, https://medium.com/the-road-to-wellness/time-vs-energy-management-4895ea33ee43

40. Isaiah 40:28-31, Zondervan, The Holy Bible, New International Translation (NIV), United States. Harper Collins, 1973.

41. Graphics, analysis, and specifications by Kelly Markey and CorelDRAW illustration by Dave Markey

Gratitude and Growth

42. Joe Biden's inaugural speech, https://www.thebridgechronicle.com/news/world/full-text-of-joe-bidens-inauguration-speech

43. Reference to critical race theory, https://abc7chicago.com/what-is-critical-race-theory-crt-common-core-math/11764262/

44. Graphics, analysis, and specifications by Kelly Markey and CorelDRAW illustration by Dave Markey

Self-Love and Self-Reflection

45. Graphics, analysis, and specifications by Kelly Markey and CorelDRAW illustration by Dave Markey

Woman of Distinction

46. Facts and figures about women, https://www.unwomen.org/en/news/in-focus/commission-on-the-status-of-women-2012/facts-and-figures

47. Proverbs 31, Matthew 7: 7- 8, Zondervan, The Holy Bible, New International Translation (NIV), United States. Harper Collins, 1973.

48. Graphics, analysis, and specifications by Kelly Markey and CorelDRAW illustration by Dave Markey

Vital Productivity

49. Workplace productivity, https://hbr.org/2016/04/the-paradox-of-workplace-productivity

50. New Zealand Prime Minister Jacinda Ardern resigns, https://www.theguardian.com/world/2023/jan/19/jacinda-ardern-resigns-as-prime-minister-of-new-zealand

51. Ecclesiastes 9:10, Zondervan, The Holy Bible, New International Translation (NIV), United States. Harper Collins, 1973.

52. Graphics, analysis, and specifications by Kelly Markey and CorelDRAW illustration by Dave Markey

Character Building

53. The true story behind the house Gucci, https://time.com/6122130/house-of-gucci-true-story/

54. The discipline of building character, https://hbr.org/2006/01/the-discipline-of-building-character

55. Photograph included with permission from Dave and Kelly Markey

Influential Finesse

56. Michael Schumacher, https://www.dailystar.co.uk/sport/f1/michael-schumacher-update-wife-corinna-27619716

57. Graphics, analysis, and specifications by Kelly Markey and CorelDRAW illustration by Dave Markey

Legacy

58. Judges 6:7, Genesis 39:19-21, Daniel 6, Zondervan, The Holy Bible, New International Translation (NIV), United States. Harper Collins, 1973.

59. Photograph included with permission from Dave Markey

Final Words

60. The neuroscience behind goals and behaviour change, https://www.ncbi.nlm.nih.gov/pmc/articles/PMC5854216/

61. Graphics, analysis, and specifications by Kelly Markey and CorelDRAW illustration by Dave Markey

Legacy Plan Checklist

62. Reference to Corrie ten Boom, https://en.wikipedia.org/wiki/Corrie_ten_Boom

63. Gender of turtles, https://oceanservice.noaa.gov/facts/temperature-dependent.html

64. Graphics, analysis, and specifications by Kelly Markey and CorelDRAW illustration by Dave Markey

www.ingramcontent.com/pod-product-compliance
Lightning Source LLC
Chambersburg PA
CBRC100735150426
42811CB00066B/1896